Pearson Education

AP* Test Prep Series

AP*HUMAN GEOGRAPHY

For:

The Cultural Landscape:
An Introduction to Human Geography

Ninth Edition

JAMES M. RUBENSTEIN

JOHN PHILIP ANTONY HURT

Social Studies Department Chair, Heritage High School, Littleton, CO

SHANNA L. HURT

Social Studies Department, Arapahoe High School, Littleton, CO

* AP and Advanced Placement are registered trademarks of The College Board, which was not involved in the production of, and does not endorse, this product.

PEARSON
Prentice
Hall

Upper Saddle River, NJ 07458

Publisher: Dan Kaveney
Editor-in-Chief, Science: Nicole Folchetti
Associate Editor: Amanda Brown
Executive Managing Editor: Kathleen Schiaparelli
Assistant Managing Editor, Science: Gina M. Cheselka
Production Editor: Robert Merenoff
Supplement Cover Manager: Paul Gourhan
Supplement Cover Designer: Victoria Colotta
Manufacturing Buyer: Ilene Kahn
Associate Director of Operations: Alexis Heydt-Long

© 2008 Pearson Education, Inc.
Pearson Prentice Hall
Pearson Education, Inc.
Upper Saddle River, NJ 07458

Printed in the United States of America

10 9 8 7 6 5 4 3

ISBN 13:   978-0-13-173210-0
ISBN 10:   0-13-173210-2

Pearson Education Ltd., *London*
Pearson Education Australia Pty. Ltd., *Sydney*
Pearson Education Singapore, Pte. Ltd.
Pearson Education North Asia Ltd., *Hong Kong*
Pearson Education Canada, Inc., *Toronto*
Pearson Educación de Mexico, S.A. de C.V.
Pearson Education—Japan, *Tokyo*
Pearson Education Malaysia, Pte. Ltd.

Table of Contents

Introduction to Advanced Placement Human Geography:

Advanced Placement Human Geography is an introductory college course in human geography. The exam assumes that you have taken the equivalent of one semester of college-level preparation, with the understanding that many high schools will teach the course for one year, depending on their schedules.

All material on the exam has been selected by geographers who are members of the AP Human Geography Development Committee. The material included in this guide correlates to what they perceive as a typical introductory college course in human geography. The exam at the end of the school year is representative of this material and is considered an appropriate measure of skills and knowledge needed in the field of introductory human geography.

There is no prescribed curriculum for this course, but rather the course gives you a learning experience similar to what you would obtain in a college level introductory human geography course. It is at the discretion of the school to develop the course to work into their already existing schedule.

The purpose of this course is to introduce you to the systematic study of patterns and processes that have shaped humans' understanding, use and alteration of Earth's surface. As a geography student, you will look spatially at the Earth to analyze humans' organization of space and the environmental consequences of their decisions. You will be looking for patterns across the cultural landscape, trying to identify trends and then anticipate future phenomena that might occur across the landscape. You will also explore different methods and tools geographers use in their science and practice.

Goals of Advanced Placement Human Geography:

AP Human Geography was established with five college-level goals in mind. These goals are aligned directly with the National Geography Standards that were developed in 1994. Upon successful completion of the course, you should have developed geographic skills that enable you to:

Use and think about maps and spatial data. Maps and spatial data are essential in discovering patterns on the Earth's surface that reflect and influence physical and human processes. Learning to use and think critically with these tools will allow you to use real world data to problem solve various situations on Earth. Thinking critically about what is obvious and also that which is hidden on various maps gives you the understanding you need to successfully use maps and spatial data.

Understand and interpret the implications of associations among phenomena in places. Geographers look at data and map sets in order to understand changes in the spatial organization of the Earth's surface. They are particularly interested in focusing on how phenomena (*an observable fact, occurrence or circumstance*) are related to one another in particular places. You should be able to not only recognize and interpret patterns, but also to identify the nature and significance of the relationships among phenomena that occur in the same place. In addition, you should understand how a culture's values and tastes, political situations, and economic conditions help to create unique cultural landscapes.

Recognize and interpret at different scales the relationships among patterns and processes. Geographic study also requires that you view patterns at different scales. Geography really is a matter of scale. You should understand that a phenomena looked at on a local scale could very well be influenced by circumstances occurring at another scale — national, local, or even global. You should look for the connections operating at multiple scales when trying to explain geographic patterns and arrangements.

Define regions and evaluate the regionalization process. Geography is not only concerned with identifying patterns across the cultural landscape, but also with analyzing how they came about and what they mean. In order to successfully make such an analysis, you need to break the patterns into smaller parts or categories, referred to as regions. By looking critically at regions of the world, you will be able to consider how and why the regions emerged and hypothesize the implications for future development of the Earth's surface.

Characterize and analyze changing interconnections among places. In order to obtain the true depth of the geographic perspective, you must understand that events and processes occurring in one place can have a profound influence on other places. You should look at places and patterns as part of a whole, not in isolation. Be aware that relationships on Earth are in constant motion, they are continually changing, and your job is to figure out how and why this change occurs.

Topics in Advanced Placement Human Geography:

I. Geography: Its Nature and Perspectives
This course emphasizes geography as a field of academic study and gives a brief overview of geography in nineteenth century Europe. This overview will show how the discipline has evolved into the study of diverse cultures and unique areas organized around some key concepts.

You will be introduced to the importance of spatial organization—the location of places, people and events on Earth. In addition, you will look for the global connections of places and landscapes in order to understand human activity across the Earth's surface.

Key concepts that will be important throughout the course are location, space, place, scale, pattern, regionalization and globalization. These concepts are essential for your understanding of spatial interaction and spatial organization of the Earth's surface. You should be able to successfully analyze human population growth and movement, cultural patterns, economic use of the Earth, political organization of space and urbanization.

You will learn how to use and interpret maps in order to make these analyses. The course will allow you to apply mathematical formulas, models and qualitative data to these geographic concepts in order to make educated predictions. The course will also ask that you make regional analysis of various phenomena and create appropriate regions to illustrate certain processes.

Ultimately, this course should allow you to see the relevance of academic geography in everyday life and decision making. You should be able to apply these key concepts when looking at current events and policies. You should be able to ask yourself the following questions: "If I were a policy maker for the United Nations, why would this information be important? How would I use it to develop public policy that would impact humans in Sub-Saharan Africa, Europe, and North America…?"

II: Population
An important geographic concept is how populations are organized over the Earth's surface. This part of the course gives you the tools you need to make sense of cultural, political, economic and urban systems. By analyzing demographic data such as infant mortality rates, crude death rates, crude birth rates, and migration, you will understand the distribution of human population at different scales: global, continental, national, state and local community. You will be able to explain why populations are growing or declining in certain places and not others. You will be asked to discover where and why fertility rates have dropped in some parts of the developing world, but not in others. Look at how age-sex structures (population pyramids) are different in many regions of the world and explain the political, cultural, economic implications of these differences. A key component of population geography that is important in today's world is your understanding of refugee flows, immigration (both internal and out migration) and residential mobility (movement to the Sunbelt) in order to appreciate the interconnectedness of our world. As well as the relationship between refugees and political boundaries, where refugees have no access to political power because they find themselves "on the wrong side of the line." Another key concept related to population is that of environmental degradation. With increases in regional population, many stresses occur on the environment, thus causing rapid out-migration and urbanization. Rapid immigration to certain parts of the world can exacerbate anti-foreigner sentiment because of the imbalance that occurs in wages, employment and political power. You will also compare different models of population change, including demographic and epidemiological transitions and government population policies. Upon completion of this unit, you should be able to evaluate the role, strengths and weaknesses of major population policies and make recommendations regarding them. For instance, is education essential in lowering fertility rates? Should females be empowered in order to accomplish this?

III. Cultural Patterns and Processes
Critical to your understanding of human geography is your ability to analyze and predict various components of regional cultural patterns and processes. In order to be successful in doing this you will be learning about the concept of culture. What is culture? What makes up a person's culture? We begin by looking at the spatial distribution of cultural

groups as defined by their language, religion, race, ethnicity and gender. It is vital to look at the past and the present in your analysis as the spatial distribution of these characteristics changes over time.

You must look at cultural patterns from a variety of geographic scales, starting with local and then looking at the global scale. Diffusion is a key concept when you are looking at these patterns. For example, you might look at where certain agricultural processes are used, or housing types, or where certain religions or languages are practiced. How did these traits get from point A to point B? Your job is to make this analysis and hypothesize just that.

In this analysis the concept of folk culture versus popular culture will emerge. This is an important way to differentiate between cultures. Folk cultures tend to be isolated and will only diffuse through relocation, like the Amish culture. Popular cultures are global and relocate through many different types of diffusion. Distinguish between a cultural groups' languages and dialects, the religious practices, and the ethnic or universalizing religions and their cultural trends, folk or popular. This will lead to your understanding of geographic patterns. You will see that each cultural leaves a unique imprint on the cultural landscape.

One important aspect of this section of the course is to look at the way culture shapes human-environmental relationships. The root word for culture is *cultus (to care for)*, so when making your analysis of what a cultural group cares about, look around. If someone would come to a major city in the USA, what would they see— NFL football stadiums, NBA stadiums, NBL fields? This cultural landscape reflects what people in that culture do with their spare time and money. Would the landscape look the same in different regions, like the Middle East or Europe? Landscapes tend to reflect the cultural values, tastes and sets of beliefs of a group of people. By looking at these landscapes you should be able to identify cultural traits, like language and religion of a group of people. This will help you to build a cultural map of the group. Where did they begin, where did they move to, where are they now, where will they be in the future?

IV. Political Organization of Space

This section of the course will introduce you to the political organization of the Earth's surface at a variety of scales. You need to keep in mind that the political boundaries that have been drawn over the years reflect somebody's view of how the earth should be divided. This view is sometimes in conflict with other's views of where a boundary should be and thus conflicts can occur.

The main emphasis is on the concept of a "nation-state" or country. How did the current world map emerge? What political entities were at play to get the boundaries we have today? You will be looking at the world in historic terms so that you might be able to analyze these changes over time. You should be able to see the relationship between colonialism on these boundaries, as well as the devolution (break up) of the former Soviet Union. You will notice that many times there is NO correlation between ethnic, economic or environmental patterns and the contemporary world map. You will consider forces that are changing the role of individual nation-states in the contemporary world, like ethnic conflicts (Tutsis versus Hutus), economic globalization, regional economic blocs (like the European Union) and the need to confront environmental issues that know no political boundaries.

In order to truly understand the complexities associated with political boundaries, you must look at the issues at different scales. That is political units above, below and beyond the state. Political units above the state level would be multi-lateral alliances, like NATO, the European Union or the United Nations. If you wanted to look below the state concept, then you would be analyzing things like, city boundaries, ethnic boundaries, voting districts, to see how groups are organized. In particular, when looking at the organization of places, understand how governmental policies, like Apartheid, can impact this organization.

V. Agricultural and Rural Land Use

This part of the course looks at four different themes: the origin and diffusion of agriculture, characteristics of the worlds' agricultural regions, understanding of why these regions function the way that they do, and the impact of agricultural changes on the quality of life and especially the environment. In order to understand the importance of the Neolithic revolution, you must identify the centers where domestication first began and analyze the diffusion of agricultural practices throughout the world. This process of diffusion makes clear the regional patterns of diet, energy use and technology that eventually emerged.

This course relies on your understanding of agricultural production regions, whereby an indepth analysis of extensive, subsistent agricultural activity (fishing, forestry, nomadic herding, ranching and shifting cultivation) and intensive, commercial activity (plantation agriculture, mixed crop/livestock, market gardening, horticulture, factory farms) will facilitate your understanding. When looking at these two types of activities, be sure to look for patterns across the cultural landscape associated with each type. You will also learn about the impact of land survey systems, environmental conditions and cultural values on these patterns.

Lastly, you will want to be able to explain why agriculture is located where it is. You will look at Von Thünen's land use model, where he explains that land rent will go down the further away you get from the center of an urban area and thus, agriculture which requires a lot of land will be located furthest from the center of the urban core. You will want to look at the impact of agricultural change (diets change when soybeans are seen as healthy now) and also the impact of distribution of crops and animals. One thing that will be essential in the future of human geography is to analyze the impact of biotechnology (genetically modified crops) on increasing food supplies and creating a globally sustainable system of agriculture

VI. Industrialization and Economic Development

This unit focuses on the economic interaction between several factors, including natural resources, culture, politics and history in specific places. By looking at each of these key concepts individually, you will be able to explain why natural resources have different values in different societies. You will be able to understand why these regions have a comparative advantage for development over others.

This unit also focuses on models of industrialization and economic development. If you understand how models of economic development, like Rostow's stages of growth where traditional societies go through five stages until they reach mass consumption or Wallerstein's World Systems (core-periphery) Model, you will understand why there is a well developed core (North America, Japan, Western Europe) which is supported by a less developed periphery (Latin America, Africa, South Asia). Identify the Brandt Line and see where this division lies. It will also be important for you to compare previously learned models (Weber and Von Thünen) in order to answer the question, "In this globally interdependent world, is time-space compression a factor anymore?" You might want to explore the role of outsourcing in order to explain the successes of certain regions, and the decline of others. Why have some Asian markets experienced a huge economic increase lately, where as sub-Saharan Africa and North America are in decline?

Lastly, you will be asked to analyze contemporary issues surrounding economic activities. How do countries, regions and local communities deal with economic inequalities? Many communities face problems when dealing with trash collection, landfills, pollution on the quality of life. You should understand the impact of deindustrialization, the disaggregation of production and the rise of consumption and leisure activities on the environment. Again, when looking at scale, you will see that there are many overlapping conditions of these problems and they are not just contained within artificially drawn boundaries.

VII. Cities and Urban Land Use
Urban geographers look at two concepts when studying cities. First, they look at where cities are located and why they are there. In this examination, you must look at the historical and current distribution of cities, as well as their political, economic and cultural functions. You will also look at the growth of cities, examining why some cities thrive, and others decline, as well as how cities are connected through transportation and communication networks. Theories are important in understanding urban growth too. One of the main theories you will look at with the history of cities is Christaller's central place theory, which explains why cities are economic hubs for surrounding communities. A region is an area with one central place, or large city, surrounded by smaller towns. In order to truly understand this idea, you should understand the rank-size rule, which says there is a specific relationship between the proportions of small towns to large cities. You will be looking at quantitative data, such as demographics, migration patterns, zones of influence and job creation strategies to analyze changes in urban landscapes.

The second concept used by geographers when studying cities emphasizes the internal structures and landscapes of cities, as well as looking at what it would be like to live and work in the city. You will look at things like urban land use patterns, racial and ethnic segregation (blockbusting, white flight), and transportation within the city, architectural patterns, and cycles of development. In this study, you will look at quantitative data, like from the census bureau, in order to identify neighborhood demographics, and also qualitative data, personal narratives or field work within neighborhoods. Here you will be concerned with models of city structures such as: the Burgess Concentric Zone Model, where cities have rings of development circling the central business district; the Hoyt Sector Model, where development comes out from the central business district, like spokes on a wheel; and the Harris-Ulman Multiple Nuclei Model, where no central business district is evident, but rather different areas (nodes) of economic and cultural development are present. (*Note: often times on the AP exam, these models may only be called the concentric zone mode, rather than the Burgess concentric zone model, it is important to know them as each.*) By looking at the architectural history and the transportation hubs of cities, spatial patterns and landscapes will become quiet evident.

You will also study current issues facing urban development today. Things like the emergence of edge cities or the gentrification of neighborhoods will be part of your analysis. You will be looking at new types of urban planning initiatives (green cities) and community actions that help shape city's futures.

Most urban geography studies focus on North American cities; therefore it will be important for you to compare urban structures in other parts of the world. The study of European, Islamic, East and South Asian, Latin American and sub-Saharan African cities can illustrate the cultural values and economic systems of different regions. This will help you to see the spatial distribution and patterns that have been prevalent throughout this course.

The AP Exam

The Human Geography examination takes about two hours and includes both a sixty minute multiple-choice portion and a sixty minute free-response portion. Each section accounts for one-half of your exam grade.

Here is the break down for each section of the **multiple-choice portion**:

Content area	Percentage goals for examination
I. **Geography: Its nature and Perspectives**	**5-10%**
II. **Population**	**13-17%**
III. **Cultural Patterns and Processes**	**13-17%**
IV. **Political Organization of Space**	**13-17%**
V. **Agricultural and Rural Land Use**	**13-17%**
VI. **Industrialization and Economic Development**	**13-17%**
VII. **Cities and Urban Land Use**	**13-17%**

When you are taking the exam, it is not wise to randomly guess at answers on the multiple-choice portion; however if you have some idea about the question and can eliminate wrong answers, then take a guess. One-fourth of the number of questions answered incorrectly will be subtracted from the number of questions answered correctly, so use your best judgment when answering the question.

Free-response portion:
You will be given three free-response prompts to answer. The questions will require you to incorporate many different geographic concepts that you have learned throughout the course. Questions may be based on verbal descriptions, maps, graphs, photographs and/or diagrams, which ask you to use your analytical and organization skills to answer the questions. It is very important that you arrange your answers the same way that the question is asked. For instance, if they have four parts to the question:

A.
B.
C.
D.

Answer the question accordingly, with A., B., C. and D. on the margin. This will help keep you organized and is very helpful for the readers, who grade thousands of exams each June.

AP Grades
Your scores will arrive in July and are based on a combination of scores on your free-responses and on the computer scored multiple-choice portion. These scores are then converted to the AP Central's 5-point scale:

AP Grade	Qualification
5	Extremely well qualified
4	Well qualified
3	Qualified
2	Possibly qualified
1	No recommendation

Strategies for Success in Advanced Placement Human Geography

1. Thinking geographically

Much of the content of this course deals with themes and issues that are integral to our world today. For example, population policies, political conflicts between and within countries, and the problems of suburban sprawl are all regular newsworthy items. The key is to think about current events in geographical terms. Students should always consider the spatial aspects of world events. For example, in a conflict between two countries the geographical importance lies in understanding boundary disputes, the location of different ethnic groups, conflict over land and resources, and infrastructural considerations. This way of thinking should be imprinted throughout the course.

2. Using and interpreting graphs, maps, and charts

The textbook contains numerous graphics, especially maps. It is critical that students practice reading and interpreting these maps. Make sure that they understand the title, key, and scale, and can describe what the map is showing. Specific graphics must be understood. For example, what does a population pyramid show? There will be graphs, maps, and charts on the Advanced Placement Human Geography examination, both in the multiple-choice section and the free-response questions. This guide includes activities and free-response questions that integrate graphs, maps, and charts so that students can practice reading and interpreting them.

3. Integrating the content

In the high school Social Studies curriculum we tend to think in compartments such as history, geography, economics, and politics. Within this course we do the same thing, and consider topics such as political geography, industry and development, and urbanization. It is imperative that students have a more holistic way of thinking before they go into the examination. For example, ethnicity and political geography overlap. Population is relevant to urbanization, and development incorporates material from other units in the course. Some of the free-response questions on the examination will require students to draw information from a number of different units, and so they must integrate the content.

4. Knowledge and use of case studies

In both sections of the examination, students will be required to answer questions that involve a specific knowledge and understanding of different places in the world. On the free-response section they may have to illustrate a concept with a specific example. Thus a working knowledge of case studies is essential. These may include the Middle East, the Balkans and the breakup of Yugoslavia, ethnic and political conflict in the Caucasus, or the political boundaries of Africa. In each of the above case studies, there are geographic issues that transcend specific chapters in the text. For example, students should be familiar with population, religious, ethnic, political, and economic aspects of regional case studies as appropriate.

5. A broad geographical knowledge

More than any other geography course, Advanced Placement Human Geography requires students to think and write critically in the content area. This should not take away from the fact that they also need to have a working knowledge of world political geography. For example, they should be expected to have a pretty good idea of which countries colonized different parts of the developing world, and the characteristics of different regions of the globe. Can students identify the major countries in each region of the world? In the context of higher level questions, the examination will still require this knowledge.

6. Knowledge and use of models

Models are integral to human geography, and students need to be familiar with them. These include the demographic transition, models of industrial location and agricultural land use, development models, and models of urban structure. Students should know the title, content, and author of the model together with the underlying assumptions. Where they deviate from reality, students need to be able to explain those differences. To what extent is the model useful in explaining spatial reality in that context? Students' knowledge of models in human geography will be tested on the examination. It is always possible that one of the free-response questions will focus on one specific model.

7. Material from a variety of texts and other support materials

This textbook covers all the key concepts and content areas of the course. The correlation guide aligns every part of the Advanced Placement Human Geography outline to key issues throughout the text. The key vocabulary terms are highlighted and defined in the textbook, and highlighted again in this guide. Together they provide the necessary content for success in the course. At the same time it must be realized that the examiners are not working from this text alone. Thus it is the instructor's responsibility to make sure that students are exposed to some other materials and texts as part of the preparation for the examination.

8. Review and exam preparation

This guide is a comprehensive review and examination preparation manual. Students need to take the practice tests under exam conditions. Each examination includes 75 multiple-choice questions and 3 free response questions. On the multiple-choice section they need to read the entire question and use a process of elimination. If they can narrow it down to two choices and make an educated guess, then they should answer it, but if they are completely unsure of an answer, they should leave it blank.

On the free-response questions, students should read the question underlining key terms, and then spend a few minutes jotting down ideas and making an outline that will help them to answer it. If a question is organized A, B, and C make sure their answer follows the same format. Introductory and concluding paragraphs are not necessary; students should get to the point quickly and be as succinct as possible. A question that asks them to evaluate involves more than one for which the task is to list. Students should use specific examples when asked to do so. On both sections of the examination they should be cognizant of the time limit.

Correlation Guide for the Advanced Placement Human Geography Units and *The Cultural Landscape*: *An Introduction to Human Geography, 9e*

Listed below are the seven units for AP Human Geography as they correlate to the key issues in each chapter of the textbook:

AP Outline	Textbook Chapters and Key Issues
Unit 1: Geography: Its Nature and Perspectives	
A. Geography as a field of inquiry	Chapter 1 Key Issue 1
B. Geographical concepts and models	Chapter 1 Key Issue 1
C. Key concepts underlying the geographical perspective	Chapter 1 Key Issues 1, 2, and 3
D. Key geographical skills:	
1) maps and spatial data	Chapter 1 Key Issue 1
2) implications of associations among phenomena in places	Chapter 1 Key Issue 1
3) different scales and relationships among patterns	Chapter 1 Key Issue 1
4) regions and the regionalization processes	Chapter 1 Key Issue 2
5) Changing interconnections among places	Chapter 1 Key Issue 3
E. Geographic Technologies	Chapter 1 Key Issue 1
F. Sources of geographical ideas and data	
Unit 2: Population	
A. Geographical analysis of population	
1) density, distribution, and scale	Chapter 2 Key Issue 1
2) consequences of various densities and distributions	Chapter 2 Key Issue 4; Chapter 3 Key Issue 1
3) patterns of composition: age, sex, race, ethnicity	Chapter 2 Key Issue 3
4) population and natural hazards	Chapter 3 Key Issue 1
B. Population growth and decline over time and space	
1) historical trends and projections	Chapter 2 Key Issues 2 and 4
2) theories of population growth	Chapter 2 Key Issues 3 and 4
3) patterns of fertility, mortality, and health	Chapter 2 Key Issues 2 and 4
4) regional variations of demographic transitions	Chapter 2 Key Issue 3
5) effects of population policies	Chapter 2 Key Issue 4; Chapter 3 Key Issue 3
C. Population movement	
1) push and pull factors	Chapter 3 Key Issues 1 and 4
2) major voluntary and involuntary migrations	Chapter 3 Key Issues 1, 2, and 4
3) migration selectivity	Chapter 3 Key Issue 4
4) short-term, local movements, and activity space	Chapter 3 Key Issue 1
Unit 3: Cultural Patterns and Processes	
A. Concepts of culture	
1) traits	Chapter 4 Key Issue 1; Chapter 5 Key Issues 1, 2, and 3; Chapter 6 Key Issue 1; Chapter 7 Key Issues 1 and 2
2) diffusion	Chapter 4 Key Issues 1 and 3; Chapter 5 Key Issue 1; Chapter 6 Key Issue 2; Chapter 7 Key Issue 1
3) acculturation	Chapter 5 Key Issue 4; Chapter 6 Key Issue 2
4) cultural regions	Chapter 5 Key Issues 1 and 3; Chapter 6 Key Issues 2 and 3; Chapter 7 Key Issue 2
B. Cultural Differences	
1) language	Chapter 5 Key Issues 1, 2, 3, and 4
2) religion	Chapter 6 Key Issues 1, 2, 3, and 4
3) ethnicity	Chapter 6 Key Issue 4; Chapter 7 Key Issues 1, 2, 3, and 4
4) gender	Chapter 4 Key Issue 4
5) popular and folk culture	Chapter 4 Key Issues 1, 2, 3, and 4
C. Environmental impact of cultural attitudes and practices	Chapter 4 Key Issues 2 and 4; Chapter 6 Key Issue 3
D. Cultural landscapes and cultural identity	
1) values and preferences	Chapter 4 Key Issues 2 and 4; Chapter 5 Key Issue 4; Chapter 6 Key Issues 2 and 3
2) symbolic landscapes and sense of place	Chapter 4 Key Issue 2; Chapter 5 Key Issue 4; Chapter 6 Key Issues 2 and 3
Unit 4: Political Organization of Space	
A. Territorial dimensions of politics	
1) concept of territoriality	Chapter 8 Key Issue 1
2) nature and meaning of boundaries	Chapter 8 Key Issue 2
3) influences of boundaries on identity, interaction, and exchange	Chapter 8 Key Issue 2

B. Evolution of the contemporary political pattern	
1) nation-state concept	Chapter 8 Key Issue 1
2) colonialism and imperialism	Chapter 8 Key Issue 1
3) federal and unitary states	Chapter 8 Key Issue 2
C. Challenges to political-territorial arrangements	Chapter 8 Key Issue 4
1) changing nature of sovereignty	Chapter 7 Key Issue 2
2) fragmentation, unification, alliance	Chapter 7 Key Issue 2; Chapter 8 Key Issues 2 and 3
3) spatial relationships between political patterns and patterns of ethnicity, economy, and environment	Chapter 7 Key Issues 2 ,3, and 4; Chapter 8 Key Issue 2
4) electoral geography, including gerrymandering	Chapter 8 Key Issue 2
Unit 5: Agricultural and Rural Land Use	
A. Development and diffusion of agriculture	
1) Neolithic Agricultural Revolution	Chapter 10 Key Issue 1
2) Second Agricultural Revolution	Chapter 10 Key Issue 1
B. Major agricultural production regions	
1) agricultural systems associated with bioclimatic zones	Chapter 10 Key Issues 1, 2, and 3
2) variations within major zones and effects of markets	Chapter 10 Key Issues 1 and 4
3) linkages and flows among regions of food production and consumption	Chapter 10 Key Issues 1 and 4
C. Rural land use and settlement patterns	
1) models of agricultural land us, including von Thünen's model	Chapter 10 Key Issue 3
2) settlement patterns associated with major agriculture types	Chapter 12 Key Issue 1
D. Modern commercial agriculture	
1) Third Agricultural Revolution	Chapter 10 Key Issue 4
2) Green Revolution	Chapter 10 Key Issue 4
3) Biotechnology	Chapter 10 Key Issue 4
4) spatial organization and diffusion of industrial agriculture	Chapter 10 Key Issues 1 and 3
5) future food supplies and environmental impacts	Chapter 10 Key Issue 4
Unit 6: Industrialization and Development	
A. Key concepts in industrialization and development	Chapter 9 Key Issues 1, 2 and 3; Chapter 11 Key Issue 2
B. Growth and diffusion of industrialization	
1) changing role of energy and technology	Chapter 11 Key Issues 1, 3, and 4; Chapter 14 Key Issues 1 and 3
2) Industrial Revolution	Chapter 11 Key Issue 1
3) evolution of economic cores and peripheries	Chapter 11 Key Issue 1
4) geographic critiques of models of economic localization, industrial location, economic development and world systems	Chapter 9 Key Issue 4
C. Contemporary patterns and impacts of industrialization and development	
1) spatial organization of the world economy	Chapter 9 Key Issue 2; Chapter 11 Key Issues 1, 3, and 4
2) variations in levels of development	Chapter 9 Key Issues 1, 2, and 3
3) deindustrialization and economic restructuring	Chapter 11 Key Issue 3
4) pollution, health, and quality of life	Chapter 14 Key Issue 2
5) industrialization, environmental change, and sustainability	Chapter 14 Key Issues 3 and 4
6) local development initiatives: government policies	Chapter 11 Key Issue 3
Unit 7: Cities and Urban Land Use	
A. Definitions and urbanism	Chapter 13 Key Issue 1
B. Origin and evolution of cities	
1) historical patterns of urbanization	Chapter 13 Key Issue 1
2) rural-urban migration and urban growth	Chapter 13 Key Issue 1
3) global cities and megacities	Chapter 12 Key Issue 3
4) models of urban cities	Chapter 12 Key Issue 2
C. Functional character of contemporary cities	
1) changing employment mix	Chapter 12 Key Issues 1, 3, and 4
2) changing demographic and social structures	Chapter 13 Key Issue 3
D. Built environment and social space	
1) comparative models of internal city structure	Chapter 13 Key Issues 2 and 4
2) transportation and infrastructure	Chapter 13 Key Issues 3 and 4
3) political organization of urban areas	Chapter 13 Key Issues 1 and 4
4) urban planning and design	Chapter 12 Key Issue 4; Chapter 13 Key Issue 3
5) patterns of race, ethnicity, gender, and class	Chapter 13 Key Issue 3
6) Uneven development, gentrification, and ghettoization	Chapter 13 Key Issue 3
7) impacts of suburbanization and edge cities	Chapter 13 Key Issue 4

CHAPTER 1: THINKING GEOGRAPHICALLY

Human geographers ask where people and activities are found on Earth and why they are found there. This first chapter introduces the basic concepts that geographers use to answer these questions. These include mapping, place, region, scale, space, and connections.

Key Issue 1—How Do Geographers Describe Where Things Are?

I. Geography: Its Nature and Perspectives

A. Geography as a field of inquiry

Geography can be divided into two major fields—human geography and physical geography. Human geography is the scientific study of the **location** of people and activities on the Earth's surface. It is the study of **where** and **why** human activities are located where they are. Geographers look at the world from a **spatial perspective**, and will study how people and objects vary across the Earth's surface. They will also study the relationship or **spatial interaction** between people and objects, as well as the movement or **diffusion** of people and ideas.

The study of human geography involves a consideration of various **scales**. Geographers will observe a tension between **local uniqueness** and **globalizing forces**. This will help to understand many of the world's problems studied in this course, including those related to political conflicts, development and economic geography, and the environment.

B. Evolution of key geographical concepts and models associated with notable geographers

The earliest geographers studied places mainly because of the necessities of trade routes and navigation. The **maps** made by Chinese, Greek, and North African scholars became the foundation of the art and science of mapmaking or **cartography**. The word *geography* was invented by the ancient Greek scholar Eratosthenes during the third century B.C.; *geo* means "Earth," and *graphy* means "to write." He also accepted Aristotle's findings that the earth was round. Two Roman geographers made key contributions to geography. Strabo described the known world in his seventeen-volume work *Geography*. Ptolemy, known as the father of cartography, published numerous maps in his eight-volume *Guide to Geography*.

Geographic inquiry continued during the Middle Ages in the Islamic world, especially through the work of al-Edrisi and Ibn Battuta. European explorers such as the

Vikings, Bartholomeu Dias, Christopher Columbus, Vasco Nunez de Balboa, and Ferdinand Magellan traveled and mapped the world beyond their continent.

Geography as a discipline developed from description to explanation and analysis through the work of two German geographers. The philosopher Immanuel Kant had placed geography within an overall framework of scientific knowledge by arguing for logical or physical classification. In the eighteenth century Alexander von Humboldt and Carl Ritter argued for **environmental determinism**, the belief that the environment causes human development.

Later geographers argued that landscapes are the products of complex human–environment relationships. This approach is known as **cultural ecology** or **possibilism**. This approach to the subject recognizes that the physical environment may limit certain human activities, but also that people can adapt to their environment.

The **regional studies** approach, which emphasizes the unique characteristics of each place, both human and physical, is a third approach to the study of geography. It was pioneered in the late nineteenth and early twentieth centuries by Paul Vidal de la Blache, Jean Brunhes, Carl Sauer, and Robert Platt. While the environmental determinist approach has largely been abandoned by modern geographers, the human–environmental relationships and regional studies approaches remain integral to the scientific study of geography today.

C. Key concepts underlying the geographical perspective: location, space, place, scale, pattern, regionalization, and globalization

D. Key geographical skills
1. How to use and think about maps and spatial data
2. How to understand and interpret the implications of associations among phenomena in places
3. How to recognize and interpret at different scales the relationships among patterns and processes

<u>Location</u>

Geographers identify location in one of four ways—place-names, site, situation, and absolute location. All inhabited places on the Earth's surface have been given place-names or **toponyms**. Place-names may tell us about historical origins, such as "Battle" in southern England, which is named for the Battle of Hastings. They can also give us an indication of the physical environment—Aberystwyth in Wales, for example, which means "mouth of the River Ystwyth." Place names may speak to religion, such as Islamabad, Pakistan, or economics, such as Gold Point, Nevada. Place-names also change because of political turmoil. The city that was Leningrad in Russia during the communist era has now been changed back to St. Petersburg.

Site refers to the specific physical characteristics of a place. Site factors such as hilltop, river, and island locations have been important in the historical origins of settlements. The site of Singapore, for example is a small, swampy island near to the southern tip of the Malay peninsula. These characteristics can be modified to a certain extent by humans.

Situation or **relative location** describes a place's relationship relative to other places around it. Singapore's relative location near the Strait of Malacca, which is a major passageway between the South China Sea and the Indian Ocean, has been key to its success as a major, internationally connected port city.

The exact location of a place on the Earth's surface can be pinpointed on a standard grid or **coordinate system**. This universally accepted system of **latitude** and **longitude** consists of imaginary arcs on a globe. Lines of longitude or **meridians** are drawn between the North and South poles according to a numbering system. 0° is the **prime meridian**, which passes through the Royal Observatory at Greenwich, Great Britain. The meridian on the opposite side of the globe is 180° longitude and is called the **International Date Line**. Lines of latitude or **parallels** are circles drawn around the globe parallel to the **equator**. The grid system is especially useful for determining location where there has been no human settlement.

Space and Pattern

Distribution refers to the spatial arrangement of something across the Earth's surface. The three main properties of distribution are density, concentration, and pattern. **Density** is the frequency with which something occurs in an area. The density of anything could be measured, but in the context of human geography it is usually population. The way in which a feature is spread over an area is its **concentration**. Objects that are closer together are **clustered** and those which are further apart are **dispersed**. Again, geographers usually use the concept of concentration in the context of population. **Pattern** is the geometric arrangement of objects which could be regular or irregular. For example, geographers could describe the regular pattern of streets in American and Canadian cities as a grid pattern.

Scale

Map **scale** refers to the ratio between the distance on a map and the actual distance on the Earth's surface. Scale is usually presented by cartographers as a fraction (1/24,000), a ratio (1:24,000), or a written statement ("1 inch equals 1 mile"). In a **small-scale** map, the ratio between maps units and ground units is small (such as 1:100,000); and since one map unit equals so many of the same units on the ground, these maps tend to cover large regions (such as a map of the United States). In a **large-scale** map, the ratio between map units and ground units is large (such as 1:5,000) and thus covers much smaller regions (such as a map of a city).

E. New geographic technologies, such as GIS and GPS

Important technologies related to geography that have been developed since the 1970s include **remote sensing**, the **Global Positioning System (GPS)**, and **Geographical Information Systems (GIS)**. Remote sensing is the process of acquiring data about the Earth's surface from satellites. This could include the mapping of vegetation, winter ice, or changes in weather patterns or deforestation. A GPD device enables one to determine absolute location through an integrated network of satellites. It also allows geographers to determine distances between two points and is thus a valuable navigational tool. GIS enables geographers to map, analyze, and process different pieces of information about a location. These **thematic layers** could include various physical features, transportation infrastructure, population, and settlement patterns, and could be analyzed individually or together. Indeed GIS is especially useful when relationships can be seen between the different layers.

Key Issue 2—Why Is Each Place Unique?

C. Key concepts underlying the geographical perspective: regionalization

D. Key geographic skills
4. How to define regions and evaluate the regionalization process

A region is an area larger that contains unifying cultural or physical characteristics. A **region** is generally defined as an area larger than a single city that contains unifying cultural and/or physical characteristics. The concept is controversial because geographers will debate what exactly makes a region. However, it is important as a basic unit of geographic research and a necessary simplification of the world for geographic examination. Geographers have identified three types of regions: formal, functional, and vernacular.

A **formal region** is also called a **uniform region** because it has specific characteristics that are fairly uniform throughout that region. For example, Colorado is a political region and the Rocky Mountains constitute a physical region. North Africa and the Middle East is a formal region characterized by a desert climate as well as Arab/Islamic culture.

A **functional region** is also called a **nodal region** because it is defined by a social or economic function that occurs between a node or focal point and the surrounding areas. For example, the circulation area of the *Denver Post* is a functional region and Denver is the node.

A **vernacular region** or **perceptual region** is one that exists in people's minds such as the American "South." When individuals are asked to draw a boundary around this region, their boundary will probably be based on stereotypes they associate with the South such as climate, accent, cuisine, and religious practices such as Southern Baptist. It would be difficult to determine the precise boundary of the South. One's attachment to a region perceived as home is sometimes called a **sense of place**.

Key Issue 3—Why Are Different Places Similar?

C. Key concepts underlying the geographical perspective: globalization

Spatial interaction and interdependence have become increasingly important concepts in geography because of **globalization**, which is the idea that the world is becoming interdependent on a global scale to the extent that smaller scales are becoming less important. It produces a more uniform world.

D. Key geographical skills
5. How to characterize and analyze changing interconnections among places

Economic globalization has led to an increase in **transnational corporations** that invest and operate in many countries. Modern communication and transportation systems have made it much easier to move economic assets around the world. Economically some places are more connected than others. **Complementarity** is the extent to which one place can supply something that another place needs. The concept of **intervening opportunities** also helps to explain connectivity. It is the idea that if one place has a demand for something and there are two potential suppliers, the closer supplier will represent an intervening opportunity because transportation costs will be less. Thus **accessibility** is an important factor in costs and interaction between places. **Transferability** refers to the costs involved in moving people, goods, and services from one place to another.

There will be generally be more interaction between things that are closer than those that are further away. This is **Tobler's First Law of Geography** or the **friction of distance**. Contact will diminish with increasing distance until it ultimately disappears. This is called **distance decay**.

As a result of globalization, there are now greater communications between distant places. **Time-space compression** describes the reduction in time that it takes to diffuse something to a distant place.

Spatial diffusion describes the way that phenomena, such as technological ideas, cultural innovations, disease, or economic goods, travel over space. The place from which an innovation originates and diffuses is called a **hearth**. **Relocation diffusion** refers to the physical movement of people from one place to another. It will be discussed later in the context of migration.

Expansion diffusion is the spread of something in a snowballing process. There are three types of expansion diffusion. **Hierarchical diffusion** is the spread of an idea from one node of power and authority to another. For example, trends in music, fashion, and art are more likely to diffuse hierarchically from one key city to another (such as New York to Los Angeles). **Contagious diffusion** is the rapid and widespread diffusion of something throughout a population because of proximity—for instance, a contagious disease such as influenza. **Stimulus diffusion** is the spread of a principle rather than a specific characteristic.

KEY TERMS

Accessibility

Cartography

Clustered

Complementarity

Concentration

Contagious diffusion

Coordinate system

Cultural ecology

Density

Diffusion

Dispersed

Distance decay

Distribution

Environmental determinism

Equator

Expansion diffusion

Formal region

Friction of distance

Functional region

Geographical Information Systems(GIS)

Globalization

Globalizing forces

Global Positioning System (GPS)

Hearth

Hierarchical diffusion

International Date Line

Intervening opportunities

Large-scale

Latitude

Local uniqueness

Location

Longitude

Map

Meridians

Nodal region

Parallels

Pattern

Perceptual region

Possibilism

Prime meridian

Region

Regional studies

Relocation diffusion

Remote sensing

Scale

Sense of place

Site

Situation

Small-scale

Space

Spatial diffusion

Spatial interaction

Spatial perspective

Stimulus diffusion

Thematic layers

Time-space compression

Tobler's First Law of Geography

Toponyms

Transferability

Transnational corporations

Uniform region

Vernacular region

CHAPTER 2: POPULATION

This chapter describes where people are found on the Earth's surface, and where population is growing. The chapter then explains why population is growing at different rates in different places. It discusses the extent to which certain regions of the world may be facing an overpopulation problem.

Key Issue 1—Where Is the World's Population Distributed?

II. Population

A. Geographical analysis of population
1. Density, distribution, and scale

The study of population geography or **demography** is very important because there are more than six billion people alive today, the growth of the world's population has been most rapid in the last century, and the fastest growth today is in the developing world. Population related issues are key to other chapters especially development, agriculture, and urbanization.

80% of the world's population lives in less developed countries in Africa, Asia, and Latin America. Three-quarters of the world's population live on only 5% of the Earth's surface. Population is clustered in the following regions: East Asia, South Asia, Southeast Asia, and western Europe. China and India each have more than a billion people and together hold over one-third of the world's population. The largest percentage of people in Asia live in rural areas, whereas three-quarters of all Europeans live in towns and cities.

The above overview of world population is at a global level and thus necessarily generalized. The analysis of population patterns at different scales, including continental, national, state or provincial, and local, will reveal different trends and patterns.

The harsh physical environments of the Earth's surface, including deserts, tropical rainforests, mountain, and polar regions, are understandably sparsely populated. The portion of the Earth's surface occupied by permanent human settlement is called the **ecumene**.

Arithmetic density (also called population density) is a misleading measure of the distribution of people because it is the total number of people divided by the total land area. For example, to say that the arithmetic population density of Egypt is 75 people per square kilometer (195 people per square mile) hides the fact that the vast majority of that country's population lives in the delta and valley of the Nile River, and much of the country is virtually uninhabited.

Physiological density is a more useful measure of population because it is the number of people supported by a unit area of arable land. The physiological population density of Egypt is 2,580 people per square kilometer (6,682 people per square mile), which is a very good measure of the pressure on agricultural land in that country.

Agricultural density is the ratio of the number of farmers to the amount of agricultural land. Countries like Canada and the United States have much lower agricultural densities than less developed countries like India and Bangladesh. In more developed countries technology related to agriculture allows a few farmers to work a huge area of land and feed many people. Thus agricultural density and physiological density are good measures of the relationship between population and resources together with level of development in a country.

Key Issue 2—Where Has the World's Population Increased?

B. Population growth and decline over time and space
1. Historical trends and projections for the future

The crude birthrate, crude death rate, and rate of natural increase are used to measure population change in a country. The **crude birthrate (CBR)** and **crude death rate (CDR)** are terms that refer to the total number of births and deaths, respectively, per thousand people in a country. Where the CBR is higher than the CDR, **natural increase (NIR)** occurs. This does not account for migration. If the CDR is about the same as the CBR a country has **zero population growth (ZPG)**. If the CDR is higher than the CBR, there is a **negative NIR**.

During the first decade of the twenty-first century, the world rate of natural increase is 1.2, which meant that the world's population is growing each year by 1.2%. It would take the world 54 years to double its population given this rate of growth; this is called **doubling time**. During the 1960s and 1970s the world's doubling time was about 35 years.

It is important to understand there are major regional differences in rates of population growth. The NIR exceeds 3% in many countries in Sub-Saharan Africa. Indeed most of the world's population growth is now in developing countries. At the other extreme some western European countries are now experiencing negative population growth. China, the most populous country in the world, has done much in terms of government mandates to lower its population growth rates. India will soon surpass China as the most populous country in the world.

3. Patterns of fertility, mortality, and health

The highest crude birthrates are in Africa and the lowest are in Europe and North America. The **total fertility rate (TFR)** is used by demographers to measure the number of births in a country. The TFR is the average number of children a woman will have during her childbearing years (ages 15 through 49). TFRs exceed six in some countries in Sub-Saharan Africa.

The **infant mortality rate (IMR)** is the annual number of deaths of infants under one year of age, compared with total live births, and is usually expressed as number of deaths per 1,000 births. IMR is a measure of a country's level of health care, and the highest rates are in less developed countries. The other useful measure of mortality is **life**

expectancy. This is the number of years a newborn infant can expect to live at current mortality levels. Life expectancy rates are sometimes twice as high in developed countries than developing countries.

Key Issue 3—Why Is Population Increasing at Different Rates in Different Countries?

B. Population growth and decline over time and space
2. Theories of population growth, including the Demographic Transition Model
4. Regional variations of demographic transitions

The **demographic transition model** explains changes in the natural increase rate as they relate to economic and industrial development. It is a process with four stages and every country is in one of them.

Stage one of the demographic transition is one of high birthrates and death rates and consequently very low growth. Most of human history was spent in stage one but no countries remain in that stage today.

Stage two is one of high growth because death rates decline and birthrates remain high. The demographic transition assumes that countries enter stage two because they go through the **Industrial Revolution**. Technologies associated with industry helped countries to produce more food and improve sanitation and health. Western European countries and North America entered stage two about 1800. Countries in Latin America, Asia, and Africa have experienced stage two much more recently, and without experiencing an industrial revolution. Developing countries have moved into stage two because of a **medical revolution**, the diffusion of medical technologies to LDCs. The sudden decline in death rates that comes from technological innovations has now occurred everywhere.

Countries will move from stage two to stage three when their crude birthrates drop sharply as a result of changes in social and economic patterns that will encourage people to have fewer children. The demographic transition assumes that people in stage three are more likely to live in nuclear families in an urban and industrial world. Chile is in stage three of the demographic transition. The drop in birthrates that comes with changes in social customs has yet to be achieved in many countries.

Countries will reach stage four of the demographic transition because their birthrates will continue to decline until the natural increase rate drops to zero. This is true of countries in Europe together with Canada, Australia, and Japan. The demographic transition assumes that this occurs because of more changes in social customs such as women entering the labor force in larger numbers.

It could be argued that some countries, primarily western and northern European, that are now experiencing population decline, have entered a stage five for which the demographic transition does not account.

A. Geographical analysis of population
3. Patterns of composition: age, sex, race, and ethnicity

23

The **age–sex distribution** of a country's population can be shown on a **population pyramid**. It will show the distribution of a country's population between males and females of various ages. A population pyramid will normally show the percentage of the total population in five-year age groups, with the youngest group at the base of the pyramid and the oldest group at the top. Males are usually shown on the left and females on the right. Each age–sex group is called a population **cohort**. Population pyramids can tell us much about the population history of a country. A pyramid with a wide base shows a rapidly growing country with a large proportion of young people, and is typical of a less developed county. A pyramid that is more rectangular depicts a country with a relatively even number of young, middle-aged, and older people, and is typical of a more developed country.

The **dependency ratio** is the number of people in a population under the age of 15 and over the age of 64, compared to the number of working people who must support them.

Key Issue 4—Why Might the World Face an Overpopulation Problem?

A. Geographical analysis of population
2. Consequences of various densities and distributions

B. Population growth and decline over time and space
1. Projections for the future
2. Theories of population growth

One of the most famous models to explain changes in population over time was developed by Thomas Malthus. Malthus was an English economist and demographer who published his *Essay on the Principle of Population* in 1798. He argued that the world's population was growing geometrically or **exponentially** but food supplies were only growing arithmetically. According to Malthus this would lead to "negative checks" consisting of starvation and disease because of a lack of food. The only way to avoid this would be for populations to lower crude birthrates.

Malthus' theory is still potentially relevant today because of rapid population growth in some LDCs. His adherents today are called **neo-Malthusians** and are led by Paul Ehrlich, who has made a similar argument to Malthus in *The Population Bomb*. Neo-Malthusians such as Robert Kaplan and Thomas Fraser Homer-Dixon have broadened Malthus' theory to include fuel, agricultural land, and other resources as well as food.

Malthus has his critics, too. The Marxist theorist Friedrich Engels believes that the world has enough resources to eliminate hunger and poverty if they are more equally shared. Contemporary critics include Julian Simon and Esther Boserup, who argue that larger populations can actually stimulate economic growth. Malthus was terribly pessimistic and did not foresee the development of new agricultural technologies or the human ability to reduce population growth rates.

5. Effects of population policies

Most demographers would agree that some parts of the world are **overpopulated**, a condition in which a country can no longer sustainably support its population because it has reached its carrying capacity. In human geography **carrying capacity** refers to the number of people a given area can support.

The CBR has declined rapidly since 1990 except in some countries in Sub-Saharan Africa. This has occurred partly as a result of economic development, which has resulted in more money for education and health care. Birthrates have also been lowered because of diffusion of modern contraceptives. Some countries, such as Bangladesh, have reduced their birthrates like this without economic development. There is opposition to birth-control programs from some countries for religious and political reasons.

B. Population growth and decline over time and space
2. Theories of population growth
3. Patterns of fertility, mortality, and health

Medical researchers have identified an **epidemiologic transition** that focuses on the causes of death in each stage of the demographic transition. **Epidemiology** is the branch of medicine which is concerned with disease. In stage one of the epidemiologic transition, infectious and parasitic diseases were the main causes of death. These include the Black Plague and cholera **pandemics**. A pandemic occurs over a very wide geographic area, unlike an **epidemic**, which is more localized. These causes of death were most common for people in countries in stage 1 and the early part of stage two of the demographic transition.

Stage three of the epidemiologic transition is associated with degenerative and human-created diseases such as heart diseases and cancer. As LDCs have moved from stage two to stage three of the demographic transition, the incidence of infectious diseases has declined. Human-created diseases are more typical of countries in stage four of the demographic transition.

Some medical researchers have argued that the world is now moving into stage five of the epidemiologic transition, characterized by a reemergence of infectious and parasitic diseases. This could be for a number of reasons, including the evolution of infectious disease microbes, poverty, and improved travel. Avian flu is one of the "new" infectious diseases that has emerged in recent decades, and it has the potential to become pandemic. However, AIDS is the most lethal epidemic of recent years, especially in Sub-Saharan Africa, where more than 25 million people were infected with HIV in 2005.

KEY TERMS

Age—sex distribution
Agricultural density
Arithmetic density
Carrying capacity
Cohort
Crude birthrate (CBR)
Crude death rate (CDR)
Demographic transition model
Demography
Dependency ratio
Doubling time
Ecumene
Epidemic
Epidemiologic transition
Epidemiology

Exponentially
Industrial Revolution
Infant mortality rate (IMR)
Life expectancy
Medical revolution
Natural increase rate (NIR)
Neo-Malthusian
Overpopulated
Pandemic
Physiological density
Population pyramid
Thomas Malthus
Total fertility rate (TFR)
Zero population growth (ZPG)

CHAPTER 3: MIGRATION

The chapter focuses on migration which is a specific type of relocation diffusion. It examines why people move permanently or migrate, both internally and internationally. Migration patterns are analyzed as well as the obstacles faced by migrants.

Key Issue 1—Why Do People Migrate?

II. Population

A. Geographical analysis of population
4. Population and natural hazards: past, present, and future

C. Population movement
1. Push and pull factors
4. Short-term, local movements, and activity space

E.G. Ravenstein, a nineteenth century geographer, identified 11 laws of migration which can be roughly organized into three main elements: the reasons migrants move, the distance they move, and the major characteristics of migration. Migration is a specific type of relocation diffusion and is a form of **mobility,** a more general term dealing with all types of movement. **Migration** is the long-term movement of a person from one political jurisdiction to another. It can include movement at many different scales, from one neighborhood to another or from one continent to another. **Emigration** is movement *from* a location, whereas **immigration** is movement *to* a location. The difference between the number of immigrants and the number of emigrants is the **net migration**.

People generally migrate because of push and pull factors. **Push factors** include anything that would want to cause someone to leave their present location, whereas **pull factors** attract people to a new location. Four major kinds of push and pull factors can be identified. These are economic, political, cultural, and environmental.

Economic factors that can lead to migration include job opportunities, cycles of economic growth and recession, and cost of living. The United States and Canada have been important destinations for economic migrants lured by economic pull factors.

Armed conflict and the policies of oppressive regimes have been important political push factors in forcing out those who become refugees. A **refugee**, according to the United Nations, is a person who, "owing to well-founded fear of being persecuted for reasons of race, religion, nationality, membership in a particular social group, or political opinion, is outside the country of his nationality, and is unable to or, owing to such fear, is unwilling to avail himself of the protection of that country." Of the more than 33 million refugees in the world, more than two-thirds of them are from Asia and Africa. There are also political pull factors such as the promise of political freedom. It was this factor that lured so many people from the communist countries of Eastern Europe to Western Europe in the second half of the twentieth century.

Cultural factors can encourage people to move to places where they will be more at home culturally. A good example of a cultural pull factor is the relocation of Jews to the newly formed state of Israel after the Second World War. Israel is the ancestral hearth of Jewish culture, and it serves as a place where Jewish people can reestablish social ties and create a sense of political unity.

Environmental pull and push factors are largely related to physical geography. People will be pulled towards physically attractive regions such as the Rocky Mountains and the Mediterranean coast of southern Europe. People might also be pushed from places by floods and droughts. The flooding in New Orleans and other Gulf coast communities in 2005 following Hurricane Katrina caused around 1,400 deaths and forced several hundred thousand people from their homes.

Migrants do not always go to their intended destination because of an **intervening obstacle**, which is an environmental or cultural feature that hinders migration.

2. Major voluntary and involuntary migrations at different scales

According to Ravenstein, most migrants move only a short distance and within a country. **Internal migration** is permanent movement within a country. This is the most common type of movement and is consistent with the principles of distance decay. **Interregional migration** is one type of internal migration, and is movement from one region of a country to another. Historically this has usually been from rural to urban, but developed countries are now experiencing more urban to rural migration. The other type of internal migration is **intraregional migration**, movement within a region. In the developed world this has largely been urban to suburban, but these patterns are now beginning to change.

One of Ravenstein's laws states that long-distance migrants to other countries usually relocate to major economic and urban centers. The permanent migration from one country to another is **international migration**, and it can be voluntary or forced. **Voluntary migration** is when someone chooses to leave a place. **Forced migration** is when someone is moved from a place without any choice.

A century ago Ravenstein stated that most long-distance migrants were male adults rather than families with children. Today there are much larger numbers of females migrating internationally together with their children, especially from Mexico to the United States. This is a reflection of the changing role of women. Much of the migration from Mexico to the United States is illegal and seasonal.

B. Population growth and decline over time and space
2. Theories of population

The demographer Wilbur Zelinsky has identified a **migration transition** which outlines changes in the migration pattern in a society during different stages of the demographic transition. According to the migration transition, international migration usually occurs when countries are in stage two of the demographic transition. For example, international migrants moved from Western Europe to the United States as a result of the technological changes related to the Industrial Revolution. Internal migration becomes more important when countries are in stages three and four of the demographic transition. According to migration transition theory, people generally move from cities to suburbs during these stages. Zelinsky theorizes that countries in stages three and four of the demographic transition are the destinations of international migrants leaving stage two counties because of economic push and pull factors.

Key Issue 2—Where Are Migrants Distributed?

C. Population movement
2. Major voluntary and involuntary migrations at different scales

At a global scale people generally migrate from the developing to the developed world. The three largest flows are from Asia to Europe and North America, and from Latin America.

More than most other countries, the United States is a land of immigrants. There have been two major eras of immigration to the United States, from the mid-nineteenth century to the early twentieth century and from the 1970s until the present. Both eras have involved people coming to the United States from countries that were at stage two of the demographic transition.

There were three peaks of this first era of immigration. They were from the time of the earliest immigration until 1840 and consisted of people largely from western Europe. The second peak was during the late 1800s and again most migrants were from western Europe, especially Germany and Ireland. The third peak was from the late 1800s until the early 1900s and consisted of people largely from southern and eastern Europe who came to work in the factories of the Industrial Revolution.

Recent immigration to the United States has been from less developed regions, especially Asia and Latin America. During the 1980s and 1990s the three leading sources of U.S. immigrants from Asia were the Philippines, Vietnam, and South Korea. In the 1980s Mexico became the leading source of immigrants to the United States. During this time people have been pushed from their homeland by economic and political conditions.

Today's immigrants to the United States are clustered in California, New York, Florida, and Texas. New immigrants often move to places where family members and friends from their home country have already migrated. This is called **chain migration**.

There have been increasing numbers of illegal or **undocumented immigrants** to the United States. In 2005 the Urban Institute estimated that there may have been as many as 9.3 million undocumented immigrants, including 5.3 million from Mexico. It is a controversial topic because although undocumented immigrants take jobs that few others want, most Americans would also like more effective border patrols.

Key Issue 3—Why Do Migrants Face Obstacles?

B. Population growth and decline over time and space
5. Effects of population policies

The United States uses a quota system to limit the number of foreign citizens who can migrate permanently to the country. **Quotas** are maximum limits on the number of people who can immigrate to the United States from one country during a one-year period. Initial quota laws were designed to allow more Europeans to come to the United States, rather than Asians. Quotas for individual countries were eliminated in 1968. The majority of legal immigration today is chain migration. Some preference is also given to skilled workers, which leads to **brain drain**, the emigration of talented people. According to the World Bank, in 2005 85% of Haitians with a college degree lived abroad.

Europe allows temporary **guest workers** to legally work for at least minimum wages in their countries. They serve the same purpose as the vast majority of illegal immigrants in the United States. Luxembourg and Switzerland have especially high percentages of foreign born workers in their labor force. Three-quarters of a million Turks work in Germany.

In the nineteenth century **time-contract** workers migrated to work in mines and on plantations for a set period of time, although many of them stayed. More than 33 million Chinese currently live in other countries. Thus it is sometimes difficult to distinguish between economic migrants and refugees.

The United States has generally regarded emigrants from Cuba as political refugees since Castro's 1959 revolution. Economic and political refugees from Haiti have not been quite as welcome in the United States. Vietnamese boat people were regarded as political refugees after the Vietnam War, when thousands fled the war-ravaged country. Vietnam remains an important source of immigrants to the United States today, but largely because of the pull of economic opportunity rather than the push of political persecution.

Immigrants often face opposition from some citizens of host countries because they are often culturally, ethnically, and religiously different. For example, there have been open ethnic and racial conflicts between citizens and migrants in western Europe and Australia in the first decade of the twenty-first century.

Key Issue 4—Why Do People Migrate within a Country?

C. Population movement
1. Push and pull factors
2. Major voluntary and involuntary migrations
3. Migration selectivity

Historically the most significant migration trend has been **interregional migration** westward in the United States to obtain cheap land and potential wealth. The population center of the United States has moved westward and, more recently, southward. In the 1960s and 1970s large numbers of white, middle-class Americans moved from the older Northeastern and Midwest to the South and the West Coast. At this time northern industrial states were known as the **Rust Belt** because their economy was declining as factories closed and people moved. At the same time the South, which had been known as the **Cotton Belt** because of its agricultural poverty, became known as the **Sun Belt**, a land of opportunity. The migration of African-Americans followed a different pattern, from the rural South to large cities in the North.

Interregional migration has also been important in other countries. Soviet policy encouraged people to move to Russia's Far North to develop industry. It didn't work very well and ended with the collapse of the Soviet Union. Brazil has encouraged people to move into the interior, especially since the building of Brasilia in 1960. The Indonesian government has paid for the migration of more than five million people from the island of Java to less populated islands.

Intraregional migration has also been important in many countries. In the United States the most important trend since the middle of the twentieth century has been the move to suburbs from central cities. A new trend in North America and western Europe has been **counterurbanization**, from urban to rural areas for lifestyle preferences, especially now that modern technology allows people to work more easily from their homes.

Migration from rural to urban areas has been very important in LDCs. Worldwide more than 20 million people are estimated to migrate each year from rural to urban areas. People seek economic opportunities with this type of migration and, especially in LDCs, are pushed because of failed agricultural systems.

KEY TERMS

Brain drain
Chain migration
Cotton Belt
Counterurbanization
Emigration
Forced migration
Guest workers
Immigration
Internal migration
International migration
Interregional migration
Intervening obstacle
Intraregional migration
Migration
Migration transition
Mobility
Net migration
Pull factors
Push factors
Quotas
Refugees

Rust Belt
Sun Belt
Time-contract workers
Undocumented immigration
Voluntary migration

CHAPTER 4: FOLK AND POPULAR CULTURE

This chapter deals with the material artifacts of culture. It will focus on the two basic categories, folk and popular culture, their origins, diffusion, and spatial distribution. Popular culture has a more widespread distribution than folk culture, and its globalization causes problems that are addressed here.

Key Issue 1—Where Do Folk and Popular Cultures Originate and Diffuse?

III. Cultural Patterns and Processes

B. Cultural differences
5. Popular and folk culture

A. Concepts of culture
1. Traits and complexes

Folk culture refers to the cultural practices of small, homogeneous groups living in traditional societies. Folk cultures are usually isolated and rural, with subsistence economies. Distinctive architecture and other material artifacts such as tools, musical instruments, and clothing contribute to the uniqueness of folk cultures. Nonmaterial aspects of folk culture include songs, stories, and belief systems. Folk cultures originate in multiple **hearths** because of their isolation.

Popular culture, on the other hand, refers to the cultural practices of large, heterogeneous societies that share many habits and characteristics. The elements of popular culture look similar in different places, and result in a relatively uniform landscape. Artifacts include music, food, entertainment, fashion, recreation, and various forms of art.

2. Diffusion

Folk culture diffuses slowly, on a small scale, usually through **relocation diffusion**. The Amish culture in the United States is a good example of the diffusion of a folk culture. Popular culture is easily diffused around the world, largely through **hierarchical diffusion**. The globalization of soccer is an example of the transformation and diffusion of an English folk culture to a popular culture.

Key Issue 2—Why Is Folk Culture Clustered?

B. Cultural differences
5. Folk culture

D. Cultural landscapes and cultural identity
1. Values and preferences
2. Symbolic landscapes and sense of place

Folk cultures are practiced by many different groups living in relative isolation. They are especially susceptible to the various ways in which the physical environment can limit their activities and diffusion, because of their low level of technology. Thus their cultural identity and landscapes will be very diverse. For example, there are many different types of Himalayan art in a relatively small geographic area because of the harsh physical environment and limited interaction. Housing provides another good example of the diversity of folk culture that results from the interaction of cultural and physical geography. The resultant landscapes exemplify distinctive and unique senses of place.

C. Environmental impact of cultural attitudes and practices

Cultural traits such as food, clothing, and housing are influenced by physical geography. Folk cultural traits such as housing are especially responsive to the environment because of their low level of technology and utilization of available resources. The sum of the effects of the local environment on a specific food item is called **terroir**. It is commonly used to describe the way in which soil, climate, and other physical features influence the character of distinctive wines. Restrictions on certain behaviors, like the consumption of particular foods, can also be imposed by social customs. This is called a **taboo**.

Key Issue 3—Why Is Popular Culture Widely Distributed?

B. Cultural differences
5. Popular culture

A. Concepts of culture
2. Diffusion

Popular culture diffuses rapidly where high levels of technology allow people to acquire material possessions. The increasingly global world allows for the rapid diffusion and acceptance of the material and nonmaterial elements of popular culture. For example, as a result of the diffusion of popular culture, there are less regional differences in housing, clothing, and food in more developed countries. Television has played a major role in the diffusion of popular culture, especially since World War Two.

Key Issue 4—Why Does Globalization of Popular Culture Cause Problems?

B. Cultural differences
5. Popular and folk culture

4. Gender

The traditional role of women in developing counties is changing as a result of the diffusion of popular culture. It is leading to the advancement of women through education and economic and social opportunities. However, it may also lead to negative impacts such as sex crimes against women.

D. Cultural landscapes and cultural identity
1. Values and preferences

The diffusion of popular culture threatens the survival of folk culture. It is one example of **cultural imperialism**, which is where people may lose their folk culture because of the influence of material elements of popular culture from more developed countries. For example, the Western dominance of the television industry, especially the news media, threatens the independence of less developed countries.

C. Environmental impact of cultural attitudes and practices

The creation of uniform landscapes through the diffusion of popular culture can negatively impact the environment by depleting natural resources and polluting the landscape. Golf courses remake the environment as do some types of commercial agriculture, and the demand for some products puts a strain on natural resources. Popular cultures such as fast-food generate more waste and thus lead to the pollution of the environment.

KEY TERMS

Cultural imperialism
Folk culture
Hearths
Hierarchical diffusion

Popular culture
Relocation diffusion
Taboo
Terroir

CHAPTER 5: LANGUAGE

This chapter discusses language, which, together with religion and ethnicity, is one of the three traits that best distinguishes cultural values. The chapter looks at where languages are spoken and why they have distinctive distributions. As well as addressing the globalization of English, the chapter also examines attempts to preserve local languages. The global distribution of languages results from a combination of interaction and isolation.

Key Issue 1—Where Are English-Language Speakers Distributed?

III. Cultural Patterns and Processes

B. Cultural differences
1. Language

A. Concepts of culture
1. Traits and complexities
2. Diffusion

The English language became a distinct language in England as a result of westward Celtic migration, as well as the Germanic and Norman invasions. Modern English evolved mainly from the language spoken by the Germanic conquerors of Britain, the Angles, Saxons, and Jutes (the word *England* comes from the *Angles' land*), and changed again with the arrival of the Normans in 1066. Modern English emerged from a mingling of French and Germanic. English diffused around the world during England's era of colonialism.

Different dialects of a language develop through isolation from other speakers of the same language as well as by interaction with other speakers of that language. English has many dialects but **British Received Pronunciation (BRP)**, the dialect associated with upper-class Britons, is recognized as the **standard language** which is the most accepted dialect for mass communication. In France the Parisian dialect became the standard form of French.

A. Concepts of culture
4. Cultural regions and realms

There are major dialect differences in English within Britain and the United States. Words that are associated with a dialect, such as the word that is used by children in Britain in a game of tag to signal that they have touched another participant, are spoken in a specific geographic region and thus have boundaries. This word-usage boundary is known as an **isogloss**.

Key Issue 2—Why Is English Related to Other Languages?

III. Cultural Patterns and Processes

B. Cultural differences
1. Language

A. Concepts of culture
1. Traits and complexes

Language is one of the oldest and most geographically diverse cultural traits in earth. Language is a system of communication through speech. Many languages have a **literary tradition**, although some have only an **oral tradition**.

All languages belong to a **language family**, which is a collection of many languages that were originally related through a common ancestor. The **Indo-European family** is the world's most spoken language family. A **language branch** is a collection of languages related through a common ancestor within a language family, although not as old. Germanic is one of the branches of the Indo-European language family. A **language group** is a set of languages within a branch that share a common origin. English is a language in the West Germanic group of the Germanic group of the Indo-European family. **Dialects** are regionally distinct versions of a single language that are distinguished by vocabulary, spelling, and pronunciation. **Ebonics** is an African-American dialect in the United States. British and American English are examples of different dialects of English. Countries designate at least one language as their **official language**, which is used for all government business. English is also known as a **lingua franca** because it is a language of international communication.

Languages of the Indo-European family are spoken on all continents but are dominant in Europe and the Americas. There are eight branches of the Indo-European family. Large numbers of people speak a language of one of the following four branches: Indo-Iranian, Romance, Germanic, and Balto-Slavic.

German and English are both part of the Germanic branch of Indo-European. The branch of Indo-European with the most speakers is Indo-Iranian which is divided into an eastern group (Indic), and a western group (Iranian). Hindi is the most spoken of the eastern group and Pakistan's principal language, Urdu, is essentially the same but written in the Arabic alphabet. The major Iranian group languages include Persian, Pashto, and Kurdish.

The Balto-Slavic languages are largely those of Eastern Europe, especially Russian. The Romance languages, including Spanish, Portuguese, French, Italian, and Romanian, all developed from the Latin language of the Romans. Provincial people in the Roman Empire spoke a common form of Latin known as **Vulgar Latin**. Latin diffused with the expansion of the Roman republic and empire, and much later, during the era of Spanish and Portuguese imperialism in the Americas.

38

There are two theories about the origin and diffusion of Indo-European. The theory of Kurgan origin states that the first Indo-European speakers were Kurgans who lived near present-day Russia and Kazakhstan. They migrated westward into Europe, southward to Iran and South Asia, and eastward into Siberia, largely by military conquest. The theory of Anatolian origin states that Indo-Europeans migrated west into Europe and east into Asia with their agricultural practices.

Key Issue 3—Where Are Other Language Families Distributed?

III. Cultural Practices and Processes

B. Cultural differences
1. Languages

A. Concepts of culture
1. Traits
4. Cultural regions

The second largest language family is **Sino-Tibetan**, spoken by nearly 20% of the world's population. It includes most of Southeast Asia and China, which is the world's most populous state. Other East and Southeast Asian language families include Japanese, Korean, and Austro-Asiatic. The final 25% of the world's population speak languages from the Afro-Asiatic, Niger-Congo, Dravidian, Altaic, or Austronesian language families.

Key Issue 4—Why Do People Preserve Local Languages?

B. Cultural differences
1. Languages

A. Concepts of culture
3. Acculturation

Thousands of languages are **extinct languages**, once in existence but no longer in use today. The European language of Gothic is such an example. Languages can become extinct through the loss of an entire people or through linguistic evolution over time. However, the pressures of **acculturation**, the adoption of cultural traits such as language by one group, are responsible for most of today's losses. Many African languages have become extinct because of the linguistic effects of European colonialism. Globalization today threatens many languages in the world.

D. Cultural landscapes and cultural identity

1. Values and preferences
2. Symbolic landscapes and sense of place

Hebrew is a unique example of an extinct language that has been revived. The revival of this language is associated with the Zionist movement and the creation of the state of Israel in 1948. It is one symbol of Israeli nationalism.

Endangered languages, such as those belonging to the Celtic branch of Indo-European, are experiencing a resurgence today. The revival of Irish and Scottish Gaelic is linked to nationalistic movements in these parts of the British Isles.

When two groups of people with different languages meet, a new language with some characteristics of each may result so that they can communicate. This is called a **pidgin language**. Where the linguistic traditions of indigenous peoples and colonizers have blended, a **Creole language** will result. This has occurred in Louisiana and is one symbol of the distinctive culture that has developed in this region of the United States.

Languages develop and change as a result of diffusion and interaction among people. The widespread use of English in the French language is called **franglais**, and the diffusion of English into the Spanish language is called **Spanglish**. However some languages lack interaction with speakers of other languages. An **isolated language**, such as Basque in the Pyrenees Mountains, is one that is unrelated to any other language family.

KEY TERMS

Acculturation
British Received Pronunciation (BRP)
Creole or creolized language
Dialect
Ebonics
Extinct language
Franglais
Ideograms
Indo-European family
Isogloss
Isolated language
Language
Language branch
Language family
Language group
Lingua franca
Literary tradition
Official language
Oral tradition
Pidgin language

Sino-Tibetan family
Spanglish
Standard language
Vulgar Latin

CHAPTER 6: RELIGION

The distribution and diffusion of major religions is outlined. The chapter also explains why certain religions have not diffused widely. The chapter goes on to discuss the relationship between religions and the physical environment. Finally, religious conflict is addressed.

Key Issue 1—Where Are Religions Distributed?

III. Cultural Patterns and Processes

B. Cultural Differences
2. Religion

A. Concepts of culture
1. Traits and complexities

As a cultural trait, religion helps to define people and how they understand the world around them. There are essentially two major types of religions, universalizing and ethnic. **Universalizing religions** appeal to people of many cultures, regardless of where they live in the world. Nearly 60% of the world's population adheres to a universalizing religion. **Ethnic religions** appeal primarily to one group of people living in one place. About 25% of the world's population follows an ethnic religion. Some religions are **monotheistic**, believing in one god, whereas other religions are **polytheistic**, believing in many gods.

Buddhism, Christianity, and Islam are the three major universalizing or **global religions**. Each is divided into branches, denominations, and sects. A **branch** is a fundamental division within a religion. A **denomination** is a division of a branch; this term is most commonly used to describe the Protestant denominations of Christianity. A **sect** is a group that is smaller than a denomination.

Buddhism is the oldest of the world's universalizing religions, with over 300 million adherents, mostly in China and Southeast Asia. Founded by Siddhartha Gautama in the sixth century B.C., Buddhism teaches that suffering originates from our attachment to the material world. The key concepts of Buddhism are outlined in the Four Noble Truths. Buddhism split into two main branches, Theravada and Mahayana, as followers disagreed on interpreting statements by Siddhartha Gautama. Theravada Buddhism is found in Southeast Asia, whereas Mahayana Buddhism is more prevalent in East Asia as well as Mongolia and Tibet. Unlike Christians and Muslims, most Buddhists also follow an ethnic religion, too.

Christianity has about 2 billion adherents and is the world's most geographically widespread religion. Christians believe in one God and that his son, Jesus, was the Messiah. Christianity has three major branches: Roman Catholic, Eastern Orthodox, and Protestant. The Roman Catholic Church, with its hearth at Vatican City in Rome, is the most important religion in large parts of Europe and North America, and is dominant in

Latin America. Catholicism also exists on other continents. The Protestantism began in the 1500s with Martin Luther's protests against the abuses of the Catholic Church. It is the most important religion in large parts of northern Europe as well as the regions of North America to which many people from northern Europe migrated. As with the Catholic Church, Protestantism also has adherents on other continents. The Eastern Orthodox branch of Christianity is only dominant in Eastern Europe and Russia, but also has adherents in smaller populations throughout the world.

Islam, with more than one billion followers, is the dominant religion in North Africa and the Middle East, as well as Bangladesh and Indonesia. Islam is a monotheistic religion, based on the belief that there is one God, Allah, and that Mohammed was Allah's prophet. The word *Islam* in Arabic means *submission to the will of God*, and an adherent is a Muslim or *one who surrenders to God*. Islam is divided into two branches: *Sunni*, which is by far the larger of the two, and *Shiite*. In recent years there has been a rise in radical **fundamentalism** that has caused more division and conflict in the Muslim world. Most fundamentalists accept the holy book of Islam, the Koran, as the unquestioned guide on both religious and secular matters. Generally Islamic fundamentalism avoids Western influence and can contribute to intense conflict.

Hinduism, with nearly 300 million adherents, is the largest ethnic religion. Ethnic religions have much more clustered distributions than universalizing religions; the vast majority of Hindus live on the Indian subcontinent. For thousands of years Hindus in India have developed a unique society that integrates spiritual practices with daily life. Hindus believe that there is more than one path to reach God; there are thousands of deities in the Hindu belief system and thus the religion is polytheistic.

The other major ethnic religion is **Judaism,** which was the first major monotheistic religion. Both Christianity and Islam have some of their roots in Judaism; Jesus was born a Jew, and Mohammed traced his ancestry to Abraham. Judaism is based on a sense of ethnic identity in the lands bordering the eastern Mediterranean. Jewish people have been returning to this land since the end of the nineteenth century, and in 1948 the Jewish state of Israel was created. Today most Jews live in Israel and the United States.

Other ethnic religions include Shintoism, the ancient ethnic religion of Japan, which is still practiced today. Some Africans still practice **animism**, or traditional ethnic religions.

Key Issue 2—Why Do Religions Have Different Distributions?

B. Cultural differences
2. Religion

A. Concepts of culture
2. Diffusion

The three universalizing religions diffused from **hearths**, or places of origin that are associated with the lives of their founders. Christianity diffused through relocation diffusion, with **missionaries** carrying the teachings of Jesus around the Mediterranean world. Expansion diffusion was also important as **pagans**, followers of ancient polytheistic religions, were converted to Christianity. It diffused beyond the European realm during the age of colonialism beginning in the early 1500s.

Islam diffused from its hearth at Mecca through military conquest across North Africa, Southern Europe, and other parts of Southwest Asia. Arab traders brought the religion to Sub-Saharan Africa and later Indonesia.

Buddhism diffused from its hearth in northern India to the island of Ceylon (present day Sri Lanka) and eastward into East and Southeast Asia as a result of missionary activity and trade.

A. Concepts of culture
3. Acculturation

Universalizing religions have supplanted and mingled with ethnic religions in various parts of the world. In some parts of Africa that were colonized by Europeans, Christianity has replaced animistic religions. In other parts of the continent, the two have merged. In East Asia, especially Japan, Buddhism and Shintoism have merged.

A. Concepts of culture
4. Cultural regions and realms

Since Roman times Jews have been forced to leave the eastern Mediterranean and disperse throughout the world, an action known as the **diaspora** (from the Greek word for *dispersion*). Many Jews have returned to the Middle East and today Israel is a Jewish state, although Judaism, unlike other ethnic religions, is practiced in many countries.

D. Cultural landscapes and cultural identity
1. Values and preferences
2. Symbolic landscapes and sense of place

Both universalizing and ethnic religions have holy places that are usually associated with the history of that religion. Adherents will make a religions journey or **pilgrimage** to holy places.

Buddhist holy places or shrines mark the location of important events in Buddha's life and are in northern India and southern Nepal. The holiest locations in Islam are associated with the life of Mohammed and include, in order of importance, Makkah (Mecca), Madinah (Medina), and Jerusalem. Holy places in ethnic religions are closely tied to physical geography. For example, to Hindus the River Ganges is the holiest river in India and they believe that bathing in its waters will achieve purification.

Universalizing and ethnic religions have a different understanding of the relationship between people and their environment. This is exemplified in their different attitudes towards **cosmogony**, the set of religious beliefs that concern the origin of the universe, and the calendar, which for ethnic religions is very much tied to physical geography.

Key Issue 3—Why Do Religions Organize Space in Distinctive Patterns?

B. Cultural differences
2. Religion

A. Concepts of culture
4. Cultural regions and realms

The Roman Catholic Church is a good example of a **hierarchical religion**, with its well-defined geographical structure and division of territory into local administrative units. Archbishops report to the Pope and each heads a **province**. Bishops report to archbishops and administer a **diocese**. The headquarters of a bishop is called a *see* and is usually the largest city in the diocese.

Islam and some Protestant denominations are good examples of **autonomous religions** because they are relatively self-sufficient, with little interaction between communities within the religion.

D. Cultural landscapes and cultural identity
1. Values and preferences
2. Symbolic landscapes and sense of place

Religion impacts the landscape in a variety of ways. Christian churches were originally modeled after Roman basilicas. Mosques are the most important religious buildings in the Islamic world, and they also serve as places for the community to gather. Most Hindus worship at home, although Hindu temples serve as shrines to one or more of their gods. The pagoda is the most visible religious architecture of the Buddhist and Shintoist landscape, and contains the relics of Buddhism.

Burial practices of different religions are also visible on the landscape. Christians, Muslims, and Jews usually bury their dead in cemeteries.

Place names or toponyms also show the impact of religion on the landscape. For example, many Roman Catholic places are named for saints.

C. Environmental impact of cultural attitudes and practices

Cremation has replaced burial as a means of disposing of the dead in many parts of the world because of the pressure on agricultural land. This is particularly true in China and western Europe. Cremation is also used in the Hindu world, although it is putting an increasing strain in India's wood supplies.

Key Issue 4—Why Do Territorial Conflicts Arise among Religious Groups?

B. Cultural differences
2. Religion
3. Ethnicity

Religious identification can lead to religious conflict. The Hindu **caste system**, which was the hereditary class into which a Hindu was placed according to religious law, has led to social and ethnic conflict in India. These issues are less significant now that the caste system has been legally abolished. The rise of communism was also a challenge to organized religion, especially in Eastern Europe and Asia.

Religious conflict continues in many parts of the world, especially at the boundaries between different religions, branches, and denominations. These conflicts have complex historical, social, and ethnic roots and must be also understood in the context of political geography. For example, there has been longstanding conflict in the Middle East. The city of Jerusalem contains sites that are sacred to Judaism, Christianity, and Islam. There have been religious wars in Ireland between Catholics and Protestants that have their origins in the English conquest of Ireland centuries ago.

KEY TERMS

Animism
Autonomous religions
Branch
Buddhism
Caste system
Christianity
Cosmogony
Denomination
Diaspora
Diocese
Ethnic religion
Fundamentalism
Global religions

Hearth
Hierarchical religion
Hinduism
Islam
Judaism
Missionary
Monotheistic
Pagan
Pilgrimage
Polytheistic
Province
Sect
Universalizing religion

CHAPTER 7: ETHNICITY

The geographic distribution of ethnicities is initially considered in this chapter. Ethnic groups are tied to particular places because members of the group, or their ancestors, were born or raised there. Another important consideration here is ethnic conflict in specific areas of the world. The attempt to retain distinct ethnic identity is one example of the preservation of local diversity.

Key Issue 1—Where Are Ethnicities Distributed?

III. Cultural Practices and Processes

B. Cultural differences
3. Ethnicity

A. Concepts of culture
1. Traits and complexes

   Ethnicity comes from the Greek root *ethnos*, which means *national*. Ethnicity is identity with a group of people who share a common identity with a specific homeland or hearth. It is distinct from **race**, which is identity with a group of people who share a biological ancestor. Biological classification by race is the basis for **racism**, which is the belief that racial differences produce an inherent superiority of a particular race. A **racist** is someone who follows the beliefs of racism. The characteristics of ethnicity derive from the distinctive features of specific geographic locations, whereas those of race are not rooted in particular places.
   The two most numerous ethnicities in the United States are Hispanics (or Latinos), at 14% of total population, and African-Americans at 12%. About 4% are Asian-American and 1% American Indian. At a regional scale African-Americans are clustered in the Southeast, Hispanics in the Southwest, Asian-Americans in the West, and American Indians in the Southwest and Plains states. At the urban level African-Americans and Hispanics are highly clustered in **ethnic neighborhoods**, especially in northern cities. At the same time these cities are also **multicultural**.
   Discrimination by race was the cornerstone of the South African legal system of apartheid. **Apartheid** was the physical separation of different races into separate geographic areas. It was instituted by the white racist Afrikaners government in 1948, and was particularly designed to subjugate the black majority by forcing them to live in impoverished homelands. The apartheid laws were repealed in the 1990s, but although South Africa now has black majority rule, it will take many years to redress their geographic impact.

A. Concepts of culture
2. Diffusion

Three major migration patterns have shaped the present distribution of African-Americans within the United States. The first was the forced migration from Africa that was part of the **triangular slave trade**. After slavery most African-Americans remained in the rural South working as **sharecroppers**, farming land rented from a landowner and paying rent in the form of crops. Blacks were still separated from whites in the South through laws that followed the Supreme Court's "separate but equal" treatment of the races. The second major migration pattern was the migration to northern cities from the beginning of the twentieth century. In these cities, African-American immigrants lived in **ghettos**, named for the term for neighborhoods where Jews were forced to live in medieval Europe. Segregation laws were eliminated during the 1950s and 1960s. The third migration pattern was their movement from ghettos into neighborhoods immediately adjacent during this time. This was made possible by "white flight" to the suburbs, which in turn was encouraged by **blockbusting**, where real estate agents convinced white homeowners living near a black area to sell their houses at low prices.

Key Issue 2—Why Have Ethnicities Been Transformed into Nationalities?

B. Cultural differences
3. Ethnicity

A. Concepts of culture
1. Traits and complexes
4. Cultural regions and realms

IV. Political Organization of Space

C. Challenges to inherited political-territorial arrangements
1. Changing nature of sovereignty
2. Fragmentation
3. Spatial relationships between political patterns and patterns of ethnicity

Nationality, which comes from the Latin word *nasci*, meaning *to have been born*, is identity with a group of people who share legal attachment and personal allegiance to a country. The desire for self-rule or **self-determination** has transformed ethnic groups into nationalities. A **nation-state** is a state whose territory corresponds to that occupied by a particular ethnicity. There are numerous nation-states in Europe, including France, Slovenia, and Denmark. However, no nation-state consists entirely of people from the same ethnic group. For example there are some German speakers in Denmark, and some Danish speakers in Germany.

Nationalism refers to the degree of loyalty that one has for a nationality. This could be instilled by promoting symbols of nationalism such as flags and songs.

Nationalism is an example of a **centripetal force**, which is one that tends to unify people behind the state. **Centrifugal forces** do exactly the opposite and may lead to the breakup of a state.

     Multi-ethnic states contain more than one dominant ethnicity. For example Belgium is divided among the Dutch-speaking Flemish and the French-speaking Walloons. They are also called **multi-national states**, and each ethnic group will generally recognize each other as distinct nationalities. This is true of the United Kingdom today with its four major nationalities—English, Welsh, Scottish, and (northern) Irish. All four field their own national soccer teams. The former Soviet Union was the largest multinational state, with 15 republics that represented 15 ethnic groups. Now they are independent states in the Baltic, Eastern Europe, Central Asia, and the Caucasus. There are geopolitical problems in the Caucasus because the boundaries of Armenia, Azerbaijan, and Georgia do not completely match the territories occupied by these ethnicities. For example, there are minorities of Armenians in Azerbaijan and vice versa. Russia is still the largest multinational state with 39 nationalities, many of which, like Chechnya, want to be independent.

     There has been a resurgence of ethnic identity and nationalism in Eastern Europe since the 1980s. Prior to this time, both were effectively suppressed by communist control. The resurgence has led to the breakup of the Soviet Union, Yugoslavia, and Czechoslovakia and the emergence of smaller nation-states. These movements for **self-determination** are fueled by **ethnonationalism**, a strong feeling of belonging to a nation that is a minority within a state.

Key Issue 3—Why Do Ethnicities Clash?

B. Cultural differences
3. Ethnicity

IV. Political Organization of Space

C. Challenges to inherited political-territorial arrangements
3. Spatial relationships between political patterns and patterns of ethnicity

     In some countries ethnicities within a state will compete to dominate the national identity of that state. This will often result in civil war. This has been the case in a number of countries in the Horn of Africa. Eritrean rebels fought against the Ethiopian army in the early 1990s and became the independent state of Eritrea in 1993. There has been civil war in Sudan for decades between the Christian and animist rebels in the south and the Arab-Muslim dominated government forces in the north. Now there is ethnic war in the western-most Darfur region. Somalia is a country in turmoil because of conflict between the six major ethnic groups, known as clans.

     In the Middle East Lebanon has experienced civil war because of ethnic and religious divisions. The country is comprised of numerous Christian sects as well as Muslims belonging to both the Shiite and Sunni sects. The island country of Sri Lanka has been torn by fighting between the Sinhalese Buddhists, who speak an Indo-European language, and the Tamil Hindus, who speak a Dravidian language.

Conflicts also arise when one ethnicity is split among more than one country. For example, there have been major ethnic disputes between India and Pakistan since these countries became independent from Britain in 1947. Even though there was massive forced migration at the time of independence, there are still minorities of Hindus in Pakistan and minorities of Muslims in India. In addition, the two countries never agreed on the location of their boundary in the northern region of Kashmir.

Key Issue 4—What Is Ethnic Cleansing?

III. Cultural Patterns and Processes

B. Cultural differences
3. Ethnicity

IV. Political Organization of Space
C. Challenges to inherited political-territorial arrangements
3. Spatial relationships between political patterns and patterns of ethnicity

Throughout history conflict between ethnic groups has led to forced migration. **Ethnic cleansing** is the process in which a more powerful ethnic group forcibly removes a less powerful one in order to create their own nation or nation-state. The case of ethnic cleansing in Bosnia and Herzegovina is a classic recent example. Bosnia was the most multi-ethnic republic of former Yugoslavia. At the time of the breakup of Yugoslavia in the early 1990s the population of Bosnia consisted of 48% Bosnian Muslim, 37% Serb, and 14% Croat. Serbs and Croats fought to unite their ethnicity in Bosnia with their respective republics; this is called **irredentism**. The Serbs in Bosnia were **irredenta** of Serbia. To do this they both engaged in ethnic cleansing of Bosnian Muslims.

After the breakup of Yugoslavia, Serbia remained a multi-ethnic state. In fact their southern **province** of Kosovo is 90% Albanian. Serbia launched a campaign of ethnic cleansing of the Albanian majority.

The Balkans has always been a region of ethnic conflict. Indeed the term **balkanized** is used to describe a geographic area that cannot be organized into one or more stable states. **Balkanization** is the process by which a state breaks down through ethnic conflict. The region is also referred to as a **shatterbelt** for the same reasons.

Ethnic cleansing led to **genocide** in Rwanda in the 1990s because of long-standing conflict between the Hutus and the Tutsis. The Hutus were farmers and the Tutsis were cattle herders. Historically the Tutsi took control and made the Hutus their serfs. The region was colonized by the Belgians and Germans and, shortly before independence in 1962, Hutus killed or ethnically cleansed most of the Tutsis. The 1994 ethnic cleansing and genocide occurred when Tutsis defeated the Hutu army and killed half a million Hutus. This conflict has spilled into neighboring countries and the region is still very unstable because of ethnic conflict.

KEY TERMS

Apartheid
Balkanization
Balkanized
Blockbusting
Centripetal forces
Centrifugal forces
Ethnic cleansing
Ethnic neighborhoods
Ethnicity
Ethnonationalism
Genocide
Ghettos
Irredenta
Irredentism

Multicultural
Multi-ethnic state
Multinational state
Nationalism
Nationality
Nation-state
Province
Race
Racism
Racist
Self-determination
Sharecropper
Shatterbelt
Triangular slave trade

CHAPTER 8: POLITICAL GEOGRAPHY

This chapter outlines the location of states and the changing face of geopolitics since the end of the Cold War. The location of boundaries gives some indication as to potential instability and boundary disputes between countries. States also cooperate with each other, and some countries have transferred military, economic, and political authority to regional and worldwide collections of states. Finally, the chapter considers reasons for terrorist attacks, and the relationship between terrorism and political geography.

Key Issue 1—Where Are States Located?

IV. Political Organization of Space

A. Territorial dimensions of politics
1. The concept of territoriality

The concept of dividing the world into a collection of independent states is relatively recent, dating from eighteenth century Europe, but the concept of territoriality can be traced to the ancient Middle East. The first states in Mesopotamia, which was at the eastern end of the ancient Fertile Crescent, were known as city-states. A **city-state** is a sovereign state that consists of a town or city and the surrounding countryside.

Later the Roman Empire provided the best example of the power of political unity. After the collapse of the Roman Empire in the fifth century A.D. Europe was divided into a large number of feudal estates. Ultimately powerful kings gained control in western Europe, and their kingdoms formed the basis for the development of the modern states that include England, France, and Spain.

B. Evolution of the contemporary political pattern
1. The nation-state concept

Political geography can be studied at a number of different scales, including local, national, and international politics. The fundamental unit of political geography is the country, which is formally called a **state**. This is an area organized into a political unit and ruled by an established government that has **sovereignty** over its internal and external affairs. This definition if a state is tested in some places, notably Korea, China and Taiwan, and Western Sahara (Sahrawi Republic). North and South Korea were admitted to the United Nations as separate countries but they both have some commitment to reunification. China has claimed Taiwan since the establishment of that country when Nationalists fled there from China in the late 1940s. Morocco still claims Western Sahara, although most African countries recognize it as a sovereign state.

A **nation** consists of a group of people with a common ethnic and political identity, but every nation does not have its own state. A **nation-state** is where political boundaries coincide with the territory occupied by a particular ethnicity that has been transformed into a nationality.

The land area occupied by states varies considerably in the world. Russia is the largest state, encompassing 11% of the world's land area. Other large states include China, Canada, the United States, and Brazil. There are also numerous very small states or **microstates**. States such as Monaco and Vatican City, both of which are located within Italy, are good examples of microstates. Larger states usually have more extensive natural resources.

At the international **geopolitical** level three theories have been important in the development of the nation-state concept in the last 200 years. In the nineteenth century Friedrich Ratzel explained the evolution of nations in his **organic theory**. According to Ratzel, states that did not expand their land area would disintegrate like an organism that fails to find food. Sir Halford Mackinder developed his **heartland theory** at the beginning of the twentieth century. He believed that the Eurasian landmass was the world's heartland and thus the key to world domination. Nicholas Spykman disagreed, and argued the **rimland** area surrounding the heartland and including the world's oceans was the key to world political power.

B. Evolution of the contemporary political pattern
2. Colonialism and Imperialism

European states controlled much of the world through **colonialism** beginning in the early 1500s. They established **colonies** by imposing their political, economic, and cultural control (especially religion) on territories in Latin America, Asia, and Africa that became legally tied to them. Technically colonialism refers to the control of territory previously uninhabited, whereas **imperialism** is the control of territory that is already occupied, but the two terms are used interchangeably.

Latin American countries became independent in the first half of the nineteenth century, and **decolonization** proceeded rapidly across Africa and Asia after World War II. Today there are only a few remaining colonies and these are generally only very small territories around the globe.

Key Issue 2—Where Do Boundaries Cause Problems?

A. Territorial dimensions of politics
3. Influences of boundaries on identity, interaction, and exchange

The shape of a state determines the length of its boundaries with other states, as well as potential communication and conflict with neighboring states.

Rounded countries with a central capital city like Poland, are **compact states**. This shape enhances communications between all regions especially when the capital is centrally located.

Prorupted states are compact states with a large projecting extension. Proruptions can disrupt, like the Afghanistan proruption which denies Russia a shared boundary with Pakistan. They can also provide access such as Namibia's proruption, which was originally designed to give this former German colony access to the Zambezi River in southwest Africa.

Elongated states, such as Chile and Gambia, are long and thin. Such states often suffer from poor internal communications.

A state that is divided into several discontinuous pieces of territory is called a **fragmented state**. The United States is fragmented because Alaska is separated from the contiguous lower 48 states. Kaliningrad is separated from the rest of Russia by the independent states of Lithuania and Belarus. Island states like Indonesia are fragmented because of water. In addition, some states have fragmented territory that lies completely within the boundary of another state. This is the case with West Berlin during the cold war and is called an **exclave**. An **enclave** is a piece of territory that is surrounded by another political unit of which it is not a part. Lesotho is an enclave because it is completely surrounded by South Africa.

States like Italy and South Africa that completely surround other states are known as **perforated states**. The states that are completely surrounded, such as Lesotho by South Africa, are also **landlocked states** that lack access to the ocean or sea.

The various shapes of states provide both advantages and disadvantages. Some states occupy strategically important locations on the Earth's surface. This is true of Singapore on the tip of Malaysia in Southeast Asia, and Panama on the isthmus between North and South America.

A. Territorial dimensions of politics
2. The nature and meaning of boundaries

States are separated from each other by borders, called **boundaries**. A boundary is an invisible line that completely surrounds a state, marks the outer limits of its territorial control, and gives it a distinctive shape. Prior to the establishment of formal boundaries, **frontiers** separated states. A frontier is a zone or area between states where no state exercises complete control. Frontiers do still exist between states on the Arabian Peninsula, where the borders are virtually uninhabited desert regions.

Physical boundaries follow important physical features on the landscape, such as water, mountains, and deserts. For example, the boundary between France and Spain is the crest of the Pyrenees Mountains, and the boundary separating Uganda, Kenya, and Tanzania runs through Lake Victoria. Physical boundaries are often **antecedent boundaries** because they were natural boundaries long before those areas became populated.

There are a number of different types of **cultural boundaries** between states. **Geometric boundaries** follow straight lines and have little to do with the physical or cultural landscape. The boundaries between many African states today are geometric. They are also called **superimposed boundaries** because they were drawn by European colonial powers that did not pay any attention to the existing ethnic boundaries between African people.

When British India became independent in 1948, the boundary that was created between the newly independent states of India and Pakistan was essentially a **religious boundary**. It separated a predominantly Muslim Pakistan from a predominantly Hindu India. It is also a superimposed boundary in that it was drawn long after the area had been settled and had established itself.

Language boundaries have always been important cultural boundaries between ethnic groups. This has been especially true in western Europe for centuries and is becoming increasingly important in southern and eastern Europe.

There are now accepted **maritime boundaries** in the world's oceans. As a result of the **United Nations Convention on the Law of the Sea (UNCLOS)**, each state with an ocean boundary has a 12-mile **territorial sea**, and a 200-mile **Exclusive Economic Zone (EEZ)** over which it has certain economic rights. Where the water distance between two countries is less than 24 miles, sometimes called **choke points**, **median lines** delimit the boundary between the two countries equidistant from each shore. Beyond this 200-mile limit lie the **high seas** that are beyond national jurisdiction and are free and open for all countries to use.

C. Challenges to inherited political-territorial arrangements
2. Fragmentation, unification, alliance
3. Spatial relationships between political patterns and patterns of ethnicity, economy, and environment

Boundaries between states will cause problems usually for one of two reasons. Conflict often occurs if a state contains more than one ethnic group. A **multinational state** contains two or more ethnic groups. The island of Cyprus contains two ethnic groups, Greek and Turkish. The two nationalities are geographically separated on the island by a buffer zone created by the United Nations. The former Soviet Union was the largest multinational state in the world, and contained 15 republics that are now independent states. Russia is still the largest multinational state because there are still ethnic groups within Russia such as Chechnya that are fighting for **self-determination** or the right to become an independent state. The pressures for independence within a multinational state from various ethnic groups are also known as **devolution** or **devolutionary pressures**. These pressures are also referred to as **centrifugal forces** because they pull countries apart.

Conflict can also occur where an ethnic group is divided among more than one state. In the Caucasus region there are minorities of Armenians in Azerbaijan and vice versa. The Kurds are a **stateless** ethnic group split among these two states as well as four others in the region.

B. Evolution of the contemporary political pattern
3. Federal and unitary states

The governments of states are generally organized in one of two ways. **Unitary states** place most power in the hands of the central government and work best in relatively small nation-states. The best examples of unitary states are those of western Europe such as Britain and France. **Centripetal forces**, such as unitary government and a strong national identity, bind countries together.

      Federal states allocate significant power to the units of local government and work well in multinational states where there is potential ethnic conflict. The United States is a federal state, not so much because of ethnic conflict but because of its sheer geographic size.

C. Challenges to inherited political-territorial arrangements
4. Electoral geography, including gerrymandering

      The boundaries separating legislative districts in the United States and other countries have to be redrawn from time to time to account for changing population. For example, the 435 districts of the U.S. House of Representatives are redrawn after the census every 10 years. This is called **reapportionment** or **redistricting**. In most U.S. states this is done by the state legislature and historically the political party in control has tried to do this. The redrawing of legislative boundaries to benefit a specific political party in power is called **gerrymandering**. The term was named for Elbridge Gerry, a nineteenth century politician from Massachusetts who tried to do this in his state, creating an oddly shaped district that looked like a salamander and that his opponents called a "gerrymander."

      There are three types of gerrymandering. "Wasted votes" spreads opposition supporters across many districts. "excess votes" concentrates opposition in few districts, and "stacked votes" links distant areas of similar voters through oddly shaped boundaries. Although the Supreme Court has ruled gerrymandering illegal, stacked vote gerrymandering is still a reality.

Key Issue 3—Why Do States Cooperate with Each Other?

C. Challenges to inherited political-territorial arrangements
2. Fragmentation, unification, alliance

      One of the most important trends in international politics is the development of international and regional alliances. **International organizations** are alliances of two or more countries seeking cooperation. The **United Nations** (U.N.) and the **North American Free Trade Agreement** (NAFTA) are both examples of international alliances. The U.N. is a global organization that focuses on peace and security, whereas NAFTA is a regional economic alliance. The **European Union** (EU) is also a regional economic union, but it additionally includes elements of political unity. All of these organizations are **supranational organizations** that include the membership of two or more states that relinquish some degree of sovereignty for the benefit of an alliance with other states.

      The **Warsaw Pact** and the **North Atlantic Treaty Organization** (NATO) were the opposing military alliances of the cold war. **Confederations** are international organizations that unite several states for a common purpose. The **Commonwealth of Independent States** (CIS), a confederacy of independent states of the former Soviet Union for common economic needs, is an example if such an alliance. There are numerous other regional organizations in the world that combine political, military, and economic goals.

Key Issue 4—Why Has Terrorism Increased?

C. Challenges to inherited political-territorial arrangements

Terrorism is the systematic use of violence by a group in order to intimidate a population or coerce a government into granting its demands. It is sometimes hard to distinguish terrorism from other acts of political violence. This is the case with some of the actions of the Palestinians against Israel, and Chesham rebels against Russia.

There have been a number of terrorist attacks against the United States in recent years but the most dramatic and devastating was on September 11, 2001. Al-Qaeda has been implicated in many of these attacks including the September 11 attack. Founded by Osama bin Laden, al-Qaeda consists of numerous cells, unites *jihad* fighters, and has used fundamentalist Islam to justify attacks, especially against the United States.

Several states in the Middle East have also provided support for terrorism at three levels. Some have provided sanctuary for terrorists wanted by other countries. They have supplied weapons, money, and intelligence to terrorists, and some countries have planned attacks using terrorists. These countries have included Libya, Afghanistan, Iraq, and Iran at various times in recent years.

KEY TERMS

Antecedent boundaries	Elongated state
Boundary	Enclave
Centrifugal forces	European Union (EU)
Centripetal forces	Exclave
Choke point	Exclusive Economic Zone (EEZ)
City-state	Federal states
Colonialism	Fragmented state
Colonies	Frontier
Commonwealth of Independent States (CIS)	Geometric boundaries
	Geopolitical
Compact state	Heartland theory
Confederation	High seas
Cultural boundaries	Imperialism
Decolonization	International organizations
Devolution	Landlocked

Maritime boundaries
Median lines
Microstates
Multinational state
Nation
Nation-state
North American Free Trade Association
    (NAFTA)
North Atlantic Treaty Organization
    (NATO)
Organic theory
Perforated state
Physical boundaries
Prorupted state
Reapportionment
Redistricting

Religious boundaries
Rimland
Self-determination
Sovereignty
State
Stateless
Subsequent boundaries
Superimposed boundaries
Supranational organizations
Territorial sea
Terrorism
Unitary state
United Nations (UN)
United Nations Convention on the Law
    of the Sea (UNCLOS)
Warsaw Pact

CHAPTER 9: DEVELOPMENT

The chapter identifies the location of more and less developed countries and then explains why some regions are more developed than others. Obviously less developed countries face much greater obstacles to development. More and less developed regions are distinguished by economic, social, and demographic indicators. Level of development varies according to gender.

Key Issue 1—Why Does Development Vary Among Countries?

VI. Industrialization and Economic Development

A. Key concepts in development

C. Contemporary patterns and impacts of development
2. Variations in levels of development

The United Nations Human Development Index (HDI) identifies gross domestic product per capita (GDP) as its economic indicator of development. Other economic indicators that help to distinguish between levels of development include economic structure, worker productivity, access to raw materials, and availability of consumer goods. GDP is the value of all goods and services produced in a country, usually in a year. The annual per capita GDP in 2005 averaged about $27,000 in developed countries and $4,000 in developing countries, and this gap has been widening. It is not a perfect measure of economic development because people in many developing countries still operate in largely non-monetary economies, and it measures average wealth rather than distribution.

The percentage of workers in the different sectors of the economy will help to show the level of development of a country. Workers in the **primary sector** of the economy extract materials from the Earth, usually through agriculture. This sector of the economy still employs the highest percentage of workers in LDCs (as much as 75% on average) whereas in MDCs it is a very low percentage. The **secondary sector** is the industrial sector of the economy, and the **tertiary sector** is the service sector of the economy; in MDCs employment in these sectors has increased. Quaternary sector jobs include business services and wholesaling, and quinary sector jobs are in health, education, research, government, retailing, and tourism. However the current practice is to consider all these jobs as groups within the tertiary sector.

Productivity is the value of a particular product compared to the amount of labor needed to make it. It can be measured by the **value added** per worker, which in manufacturing is the gross value of the product minus the costs of raw materials and energy. Productivity is much higher in MDCs because of higher technology and capital intensive industries. Production in LDCs is still very labor intensive.

Development requires access to raw materials, although some developed countries such as Japan, Singapore, and Switzerland lack significant resources; some developing countries such as those in Sub-Saharan Africa have significant raw materials. Development also requires energy to fuel industry and transform raw materials into finished products.

Countries that produce more quality nonessential consumer goods are able to promote expansion of industry and the generation of additional wealth. Consumer goods such as automobiles, telephones, and televisions are very accessible to many people in MDCs but only to the few who are wealthy in LDCs.

Education and health are key social indicators of development. High levels of development are associated with high levels of education. The quality of education is typically measured by student/teacher ratio and literacy rates. The **literacy rate** is the percentage of a country's population who can read and write. Literacy rates in MDCs usually exceed 98%, whereas many LDCs have rates that are below 60%. There are also huge differences between literacy rates for men and women in developing countries. People are also healthier in more developed countries because they have better nutrition and access to health care.

The United Nations' HDI includes life expectancy as a measure of development. Other demographic indicators include infant mortality, natural increase, and crude birthrates. Life expectancy is a measure of health and welfare; some developed countries have life expectancies that are twice as high as developing countries. Infant mortality rates speak to levels of health care in a country. Rates of natural increase are much higher in LDCs and force them to allocate increasing percentages of their GDPs to care for a rapidly expanding population. Developing countries have higher rates of natural increase because they have higher crude birthrates. One has to be careful when looking at crude death rates to help measure levels of development for two reasons. Firstly the diffusion of medical technology from MDCs to LDCs has reduced death rates in less developed countries. Secondly the high crude death rates of some MDCs are a reflection of their higher percentages of elderly and lower percentages of children.

Key Issue 2—Where Are More and Less Developed Countries Distributed?

A. Key concepts in development

Development is the process of economic growth, in which countries try to improve their level of material wealth through the diffusion and realization of resources, knowledge, and technology. It is a continuous process and each country lies somewhere along that continuum. A **more developed country** (**MDC**, and also known as a **developed country**) will be further along that continuum than a **less developed country** (**LDC**, and also known as a **developing country**).

The **Human Development Index** (**HDI**) is one measure of development. It was created by the United Nations and calculates development in terms of human welfare rather than money or productivity. It evaluates human welfare in three areas: economic, social, and demographic. The economic factor is **gross domestic product** per capita

(GDP); the social factors are the **literacy rate** and amount of education; and the demographic factor is life expectancy. The highest HDI possible is 1.0 or 100% and the countries of the world can be categorized into nine regions according to their level of development.

C. Contemporary patterns and impacts of industrialization and development
1. Spatial organization of the world economy
2. Variations in levels of development

Five of the nine regions identified by the United Nations HDI are more developed. These include Anglo-America, western and eastern Europe, Japan, and the South Pacific. Anglo-America has the highest HDI (0.94) and is well endowed with natural resources and agricultural land. It has developed high-tech industries, and is a leading consumer and the world's largest market.

Western Europe has a very high HDI (0.93). It must buy many raw materials from other countries but it has developed economies around high-value goods and services industries to offset these imports. Western Europe has offset the potential disadvantages of a history of conflict and cultural diversity by creating the European Union, which is potentially the world's largest and richest market.

Eastern Europe has the lowest HDI of these five regions (0.80) and is the only region where the HDI has actually declined in recent years. This is the result of the legacy of communist rule. The region's HDI has declined because of the economic vacuum created by the end of communist rule together with higher death rates. Many central European countries have made the transition to market economies and have benefited from closer ties to the European Union. However, other countries, especially those from the former Soviet Union and Yugoslavia, continue to languish.

Japan has become a great economic power despite lacking key resources. It has developed a skilled labor force that specializes in high-quality and high-value products. Australia and New Zealand share many cultural characteristics with Britain, although their economies, which are net exporters of food and other resources, are increasingly tied to Asian countries.

The six regions that can be classified as developing are Latin America, East Asia, the Middle East, Southeast Asia, South Asia, and Sub-Saharan Africa in order of development level.

A higher percentage of people in Latin America, with an HDI of 0.80, live in urban areas than any other developing region. Development in this region is also characterized by tremendous inequality in income distribution. In East Asia, which has an HDI of 0.76, China is now the world's second largest economy, and the largest market for consumer products. Manufacturing has moved to this region because of low wages which is driving down factory pay around the world. There are also regional economic equalities in China.

The harsh physical environment of the Middle East, with an HDI of 0.68, does not support high population concentrations but the region has the largest percentage of the world's petroleum reserves. This allows many countries in the region to enjoy a trade surplus and use petroleum wealth to finance economic development. However there is a large gap in per capita income between the petroleum-rich countries and those that lack resources. These countries have to deal with traditional cultural values associated with Islam which can hinder development, especially where the role of women is concerned. The United Nations has constructed an Alternative Human Development Index for Middle Eastern countries that identifies three reasons for the region's relatively low HDI—lack of political freedom, low education and literacy rates, and lack of opportunities for women.

Indonesia, Vietnam, and Thailand are the most populous countries in Southeast Asia, a region that concentrates on the production of agricultural products that are used in manufacturing. Some countries in this region, including Thailand, Singapore, Malaysia, and the Philippines, have developed rapidly, especially because of growing manufacturing built on cheap labor. South Asia has the second-highest population and the second-lowest per capita income. India is one of the world's leading rice and wheat producers thanks in large part to the innovations of the Green Revolution. It now has the world's fourth largest economy.

With an HDI of 0.51, Sub-Saharan Africa is the poorest region in the world, although it is a major source of mineral wealth. Many of the region's economic and political problems are legacies of the colonial era.

Key Issue 3—Where Does Level of Development Vary by Gender?

A. Key concepts in development

C. Contemporary patterns and impacts of industrialization and development
2.Variations in levels of development

The **Gender-Related Development Index (GDI)** uses the same indicators of development to reflect differences in the accomplishments and conditions of men and women. A country with complete gender equality would have a GDI of 1.0. According to 2005 data Norway has the highest GDI (0.960) which means that both men and women in this country have achieved a high level of development. The lowest GDIs, where women's level of development is substantially below that of men, are in Sub-Saharan Africa.

Women on average have two-thirds of the income of men in MDCs. The disparity is less in dollar terms in LDCs. The gap between men and women in education and literacy is much greater in LDCs than in MDCs. When it comes to life expectancy, the gender gap is greater in MDCs than in LDCs.

The **Gender Empowerment Measure (GEM)** measures the degree of economic and political power held by women. The GEM economic indicator is the percentage of women in professional and technical jobs. This indicator is much higher in MDCs than in LDCs. One indicator of the political power of women is the percentage of the country's administrative and managerial jobs they hold. This is higher in MDCs, especially Europe, than LDCs. The other political indicator of empowerment is the percentage of women elected to public office. The highest percentages are in northern Europe, and every country has a lower GEM than GDI.

Key Issue 4—Why Do Less Developed Countries Face Obstacles to Development?

B. Growth and diffusion of industrialization
4. Geographic critiques of models of economic localization

For much of the twentieth century self-sufficiency or balanced growth was the most popular development alternative, especially for LDCs. It protects infant industries by setting barriers and tariffs on imports, as well as fixing quotas and requiring licenses to restrict the number of legal importers. India followed this model of development in the decades after independence from Britain. It has two major problems. It protects inefficient industries and creates a large bureaucracy to administer the various controls.

Development through international trade takes a very different approach. By following this approach a country can develop its unique economic assets and use the funds from these exports to finance other development.

In the 1950s W.W. Rostow proposed his **development model**, which helped countries to move towards development through international trade. This was a five-stage model. Stage one is a traditional society, in which a country is still predominantly agricultural. In stage two a country reaches the preconditions for takeoff when entrepreneurs initiate economic activities. Infrastructure develops and productivity increases. Stage three is takeoff, which is essentially the beginning of an industrial revolution. In the drive to maturity stage, industry diffuses and results in rapid growth. According to Rostow, the final stage is the age of mass consumption, when the economy shifts from heavy industry to the production of consumer goods. This model was based on the belief that MDCs in western Europe and Anglo-America would be followed by countries in eastern Europe and Japan. Also, many LDCs have an abundance of raw materials that would generate funds to promote development in these countries.

The international trade approach has been followed by numerous countries in Asia. The most successful initially in Asia included South Korea, Singapore, Taiwan and Hong Kong (then a British colony). They concentrated on the production of manufacturing goods using cheap labor. The petroleum-rich Arab countries pursued the same approach. Saudi Arabia, Kuwait, Bahrain, Oman, and the United Arab Emirates have been very successful, using petroleum revenues to finance large-scale projects.

The international trade approach to development also has problems. These include uneven resource distribution, market stagnation, and increased dependence on MDCs. But it has now been embraced by most countries. This approach has been aided by the creation of the **World Trade Organization (WTO)** in 1995, which helps to reduce barriers to international trade. The WTO helps to eliminate trade restrictions between countries. It also enforces international trade agreements.

Investment made by **transnational corporations (TNCs)** in foreign countries is known as **foreign direct investment (FDI)**. The headquarters of most TNCs are in the United States and western Europe.

LDCs borrow money for major projects from two major international lenders. The **World Bank** includes the International Bank for Reconstruction and Development (IBRD) and the International Development Association (IDA). They provide loans for the

65

reform of public administration and legal institutions. The **International Monetary Fund (IMF)** provides loans to countries that have balance-of-payment problems rather than for specific projects. There are numerous problems associated with all of these loans. Many new projects in LDCs are expensive failures, and many LDCs have been unable to repay interest and loans. Neither of these organizations will cancel or refinance debts without strings attached. Before granting debt relief, an LDC is required to prepare a Policy Framework Paper (PFP) outlining a **structural adjustment program** that includes economic goals and strategies for achieving the objectives.

Fair trade has been proposed as an alternative to the international trade model of development. **Fair trade** means that products are made and traded according to standards that protect workers and small businesses in LDCs. Standards for fair trade are set internationally by Fairtrade Labelling Organizations International (FLO). Ten Thousand Villages, which specializes in handicrafts, is the largest fair trade organization in North America. Two sets of standards distinguish fair trade; one set applies to workers on farms and in factories and the other to producers.

The world is clearly divided into regions that have differing levels of economic development. The **core–periphery model** explains this in a simplified way. The wealthiest countries are the core and the less developed countries are on the periphery. There are some countries, such as Chile, Brazil, and China, that don't easily fit into either and are thus sometimes described as **semi-peripheral**.

Immanuel **Wallerstein's World Systems Theory** is similar to the core–periphery model. Wallerstein believed that the concept of core–periphery developed in the fifteenth century as Europeans began to explore and control the globe. His theory describes the world as an interdependent system of countries.

KEY TERMS

Core–periphery model
Developed country
Developing country
Development
Fair trade
Foreign direct investment
Gender Empowerment Measure (GEM)
Gender-Related Development Index
    (GDI)
Gross domestic product (GDP)
Human Development Index (HDI)
International Monetary Fund (IMF)
Less developed country (LDC)
Literacy rate
More developed country (MDC)
Primary sector
Productivity
Rostow's Development Model

Secondary sector
Semi-periphery
Structural adjustment program
Tertiary sector
Transnational corporation
Value added
Wallerstein's World Systems Theory
World Bank
World Trade Organization (WTO)

CHAPTER 10: AGRICULTURE

This chapter deals with the major primary sector economic activity—agriculture. The origins and diffusion of agriculture are considered first. Farming varies around the world because of a variety of cultural and physical environmental factors. Agriculture is very different in less and more developed regions. In less developed regions, dominated by subsistence agriculture, farm products are usually consumed near to where they are produced. Commercial farming is the norm in more developed countries and farmers sell what they produce. Farmers face numerous problems in each type of region.

Key Issue 1—Where Did Agriculture Originate?

V. Agriculture and Rural Land Use

A. Development and diffusion of agriculture
1. Neolithic Agricultural Revolution

Prior to the invention of agriculture, humans lived as nomadic **hunters and gatherers**, traveling in small groups and collecting food daily. Over thousands of years plant cultivation evolved through a combination of accident and deliberate experiment. In this way, about 10,000 years ago, people started to practice **agriculture**, the deliberate modification of the Earth's surface through the cultivation of plants and **domestication** of animals, for sedentary food production. The word *cultivate* means "to care for," and a **crop** is any plant cultivated by people.

According to the geographer Carl Sauer, there were two initial types of cultivation. The first was **vegetative planting**, which is the reproduction of plants by direct cloning from existing plants. **Seed agriculture** came later; this is the reproduction of plants through seeds. This is practiced by most farmers today.

There were probably a number of agricultural hearths for both vegetative planting and seed agriculture. Sauer believes that vegetative planting originated in Southeast Asia and diffused from there to other parts of Asia, the Middle East, Africa, and southern Europe. There may have been other independent vegetative hearths in west Africa and South America.

Sauer identified numerous hearths for seed agriculture, in Asia, Africa, and the Americas. Agriculture had multiple hearths because, to a certain extent, the physical environment determines the food that will be produced.

A. Development and diffusion of agriculture
2. Second Agricultural Revolution

B. Major agricultural production regions

D. Modern commercial agriculture

4. Spatial organization and diffusion of industrial agriculture

In **subsistence agriculture**, found in less developed countries (LDCs), farmers produce goods to provide for themselves. **Commercial agriculture**, found in more developed countries (MDCs), is the production of food for competitive, free market sale. This type of agriculture emerged as a result of increased farming technology that was developed during the **Second Agricultural Revolution** in the years preceding the Industrial Revolution in eighteenth century Europe. In **planned agricultural economies**, such as communist countries, the government controls every phase of agricultural production.

Five principal features distinguish commercial from subsistence agriculture. Firstly, as mentioned above, the purpose of farming is different in LDCs and MDCs. Secondly, agriculture in LDCs is more **labor-intensive** than the **capital-intensive** agriculture which is the norm in MDCs. Thus there will always be a higher percentage of the labor force involved in agriculture in the developing world. Thirdly and related to the percentage of farmers in the labor force, agriculture in developed countries involves more machinery and technology. Fourthly, farm size is larger in commercial agriculture, especially in the United States and Canada. The loss of very productive farmland, known as **prime agricultural land**, is an increasing problem in the United States because of urban sprawl. Finally, in commercial agriculture there is a close relationship between agriculture and other businesses. This is not the case in subsistence agriculture. In developed countries the system of commercial farming is called **agribusiness** because farming is integrated into a large food production industry.

Key Issue 2—Where Are Agricultural Regions in Less Developed Countries?

B. Major agricultural production regions
1. Agricultural systems associated with major bioclimatic zones

Shifting cultivation is practiced in much of the world's tropical regions. Farmers clear land for planting by slashing vegetation and burning the debris; this is called **slash and burn agriculture**. The cleared land is called **swidden** and crops grown will include rice (Asia), maize and manioc (South America), millet and sorghum (Africa). Farmers will only grow crops on a cleared field for a few years until the soil nutrients are depleted and then they will leave it **fallow** (nothing planted) so that it can recover. This type of agriculture occupies about one quarter of the world's land area but only supports about 5% of the world's population. As rainforests are being cut, shifting cultivation is being cut; especially in the Amazon basin, shifting cultivation is being replaced by logging, cattle ranching, and cash crops.

Pastoral nomadism is another type of **extensive subsistence agriculture** that involves nomadic **animal husbandry**. It is practiced in the dry climates of the developing world. The livestock provide food, clothing, and shelter. The animals will vary depending on cultural preferences and physical geography but may include goats, camels, horses, sheep, or cattle. Pastoral nomads have a strong sense of territoriality which determines the land that they occupy. Some pastoral nomads practice **transhumance**, which is the

68

seasonal movement of livestock between mountains and lowland pasture areas. **Pasture** is grass or other plants grown for feeding livestock, as well as land used for grazing. This type of agricultural system is on the decline as modern technology is resulting in the conversion of land from nomadic to sedentary agriculture.

Some subsistence agriculture is **intensive**, where farmers work land more intensively to subsist. **Intensive subsistence agriculture** is practiced in much of Asia on small plots and mostly by hand. **Wet rice** is the dominant crop in Southeast Asia, including China. Wet rice is planted in dry soil in a nursery and then moved to seedlings in a flooded field. The flooded field is called a **sawah** (**paddy** is the Malay word for wet rice).When the rice is harvested the husks, known as **chaff**, are separated from the seeds when their heads are **threshed** by being beaten on the ground. When the threshed rice is placed on a tray, the lighter chaff is **winnowed** or blown away by the wind. If the rice is to be consumed by the farmer, the **hull**, or outer covering, is removed by mortar and pestle. In parts of Asia farmers can get two harvests per year from one field. This is known as **double cropping**. Where wet rice is not dominant in Asia, more than one harvest can be obtained each year through **crop rotation**, which is the practice of using different fields from crop to crop each year to avoid soil exhaustion.

Plantation agriculture is the only significant large-scale commercial agriculture in the developing world. Plantations will specialize in crops that will usually be exported to other countries such as sugarcane and coffee. They have typically been owned by foreign companies and are very labor intensive.

Key Issue 3—Where Are Agricultural Regions in More Developed Countries?

B. Major agricultural production regions
1. Agricultural systems associated with major bioclimatic zones

D. Modern commercial agriculture
4. Spatial organization and diffusion of industrial agriculture

Mixed crop and livestock farming is practiced in much of the United States and northern Europe. Most of the crops are fed to animals. Corn is generally the crop of choice because of its high yields per area, followed by soybeans.

Dairy farming is an important type of commercial agriculture near urban areas in North America and Europe, where it accounts for about 20% of the total value of agricultural output. Australia and New Zealand also have major dairy production regions. The ring surrounding a city from which milk can be supplied without spoiling is called the **milkshed**. Increasingly in the developed world, thanks to modern transportation systems, dairy production can take place further from the market.

Commercial grain farming, which includes wheat and corn, takes place in western North America and southern Russia. In North America there is a **winter wheat** belt in Kansas, Colorado, and Oklahoma, where the crop is planted in the autumn. In the **spring wheat** belt, which includes the Dakotas, Montana, and southern Saskatchewan, the crop is planted in the spring. A third important grain growing region is in the state of Washington. Large-scale wheat production was first made possible by the McCormick

reaper in the 1830s. Today the **combine** performs the three tasks of reaping, threshing, and cleaning in one operation.

Livestock ranching is the extensive commercial grazing of livestock land in semiarid or arid lands. It is practiced in much of the western United States and the pampas regions of Argentina, southern Brazil, and Uruguay. Historically ranching involved the herding of cattle over open ranges in a semi-nomadic style, and later became sedentary farming by dividing open land into ranches. Today it has become part of the meat-processing industry rather than an economic activity practiced on isolated farms.

Mediterranean agriculture, practiced in the Mediterranean, California, and parts of Chile, Australia, and South Africa, consists of diverse crops such as grapes, olives, nuts, fruits, and vegetables, mostly for human consumption. **Horticulture** is the term for the growing of fruits, vegetables, and flowers.

Commercial gardening and fruit farming is the dominant form of agriculture in the southeastern United States. It is practiced close to urban areas and is also called **truck farming** because "truck" was the Middle English word for barter or the exchange of commodities. Truck farms grow fruits and vegetables.

C. Rural land use and settlement patterns
1. Models of agricultural land use, including von Thünen model

The **von Thünen model** helps to explain the importance of proximity to market and the choice of crops in commercial agriculture. Johann von Thünen published his model in a book titled *The Isolated State* in 1826. According to von Thünen, rent, or land value, will decrease the further one gets from a market. Thus the agricultural products that use the land most intensively, have the highest transportation costs, are more perishable, and are in the greatest demand, such as dairying and fruits and vegetables, will be located close to the market. Agriculture that uses the land more extensively, such as livestock ranching, will be further away from the market.

Von Thünen placed horticulture and dairying closest to the city, followed by forestry (for fuel and building). The next rings were used for various crops and pasture, becoming more extensive further from the market. The model had various assumptions that may not have been true in reality, such as a uniform landscape, equal ease of transportation in all directions, and a single market.

Although *The Isolated State* is a dated and oversimplified model of reality, the principles of agricultural location still apply today, especially at a national or global scale, and it still describes the actual patterns of land use surrounding many cities.

Key Issue 4—Why Do Farmer Face Economic Difficulties?

B. Major agricultural production regions
2. Variations within major zones and effects of markets

D. Modern commercial agriculture
3. Biotechnology

Agricultural regions are largely determined by climate and, to a lesser extent, cultural preferences. In addition, there are two important economic considerations for subsistence farmers. These are rapid population growth and the demands of the international market.

According to Esther Boserup, as population has increased in subsistence economies, farmers have intensified production by leaving land fallow for shorter periods and by the adoption of new farming methods.

In some LDCs such as Kenya, families may divide by gender between traditional subsistence agriculture and the growing of crops for export. Women practice most of the subsistence agriculture while men grow crops for export, one of the legacies of colonial agricultural systems, or work in urban jobs. The export crops grown in some LDCs, especially in Latin America and Asia, are those that can be converted to drugs.

Sub-Saharan African countries have been encouraged by the United States to increase their food supply in part by increased use of **genetic modification (GM)** of crops and livestock, which could increase yields and nutrition and provide more resistance to pests.

Overproduction is a problem in commercial farming, especially in the United States and Europe. Even though demand has remained constant, the U.S. government has tried to alleviate the problem by encouraging the planting of fallow crops, subsidizing farmers, and purchasing surplus production.

Sustainable agriculture is becoming more widespread in MDCs. This type of agriculture promotes environmental quality through sensitive land management, limited use of chemicals, and integrating the growing of crops and raising of livestock. One type of land management is **ridge tillage**, which is the planting of crops on ridge tops to conserve soil.

B. Major agricultural production regions
3. Linkages and flows among regions of food production and consumption

D. Modern commercial agriculture
1. Third agricultural revolution
2. Green revolution
5. Future food supplies and environmental impacts of agriculture

Food supply can be increased in the world by initiating a number of strategies. Expansion of land under production is one method, although this can lead to environmental problems such as **desertification** in arid regions. Soil salinity has also been a problem where irrigated agriculture is practiced in hot, arid regions. The **green revolution** (also known as the third agricultural revolution), which involved the use of new higher-yield seeds as well as fertilizers during the 1970s and 1980s, has resulted in increased food supply in parts of Asia and Latin America. Strategies are now being developed to expand **aquaculture,** fish farming or the cultivation of the oceans. Higher-protein cereals are being developed in MDCs, and the palatability of rarely consumed foods, like soybean, is being improved. Another alternative for increasing the world's

71

food supply is to export more food from MDCs that produce surpluses to LDCs, especially in Africa, that are experiencing a food-supply crisis.

KEY TERMS

Agribusiness
Agriculture
Animal husbandry
Aquaculture
Capital-intensive
Cereal grain
Chaff
Combine
Commercial agriculture
Commercial gardening and fruit farming
Commercial grain farming
Crop
Crop rotation
Dairy farming
Desertification
Domestication
Double cropping
Extensive subsistence agriculture
Fallow
Genetic modification (GM)
Grain
Green revolution
Horticulture
Hull
Hunters and gatherers
Intensive subsistence agriculture
Labor-intensive
Livestock ranching
Mediterranean agriculture

Milkshed
Mixed crop and livestock farming
Paddy
Pastoral nomadism
Pasture
Planned agricultural economies
Plantation
Prime agricultural land
Ranching
Reaper
Ridge tiller
Sawah
Second Agricultural Revolution
Seed agriculture
Slash-and-burn agriculture
Shifting cultivation
Spring wheat
Subsistence agriculture
Sustainable agriculture
Swidden
Thresh
Transhumance
Truck farming
Vegetative planting
von Thünen Model
Wet rice
Winnow
Winter wheat

CHAPTER 11: INDUSTRY

This chapter outlines the regions where industry is located and why. The two most important considerations regarding location are where the markets for the products are located and where the necessary resources are located. Increasingly industry has diffused from MDCs to LDCs, especially through the operation of transnational corporations.

Key Issue 1—Where Is Industry Distributed?

VI. Industrialization and Economic Development

B. Growth and diffusion of industrialization
2. Industrial Revolution

The **Industrial Revolution** originated in Britain during the late eighteenth century because of the combination of entrepreneurs, capital, raw materials, and available labor. It also included social and political changes but it generally refers to the economic changes that began in Britain in the late 1700s.

B. Growth and diffusion of industrialization
1. The changing role of energy and technology
3. Evolution of economic cores and peripheries

C. Contemporary patterns and impacts of industrialization and development
1. Spatial organization of the world economy

Three-quarters of the world's industrial production is concentrated in four regions: northwestern Europe, eastern Europe, eastern North America, and East Asia.

Western Europe has major industrialization regions in Britain, the Rhine-Ruhr Valley, the mid-Rhine, and northern Italy. Britain's is the oldest of these industrial regions, although it is now attracting high-tech industries, especially Japanese companies. Most British industries locate in southeast England today. The Rhine-Ruhr has been important largely because of coal and iron deposits and steelmaking. The mid-Rhine includes parts of Germany and France and has been important because of its proximity to large consumer markets. The Po valley of northern Italy began with **textile** manufacturing and has benefited from low labor costs.

The oldest industrial areas in eastern Europe are the central industrial district, which is centered on Moscow, and the St. Petersburg industrial district, which was one of Russia's early nodes of industrial development. Other industrial areas in eastern Europe include the Volga industrial district, particularly important for petroleum and natural gas, and the Ural industrial district, which has become a main source of raw materials but lacks energy sources. The Kuznetsk is Russia's most important industrial region east of the Ural Mountains. Outside the former Soviet Union there are important industrial regions in eastern Ukraine and Silesia, which includes parts of Poland and the Czech Republic.

North America became a major industrial region later than Europe. Textiles were important in the United States by 1860. Manufacturing has been traditionally located in the northeastern United States with its numerous raw materials. These areas include New England, the Middle Atlantic, the Mohawk Valley, and the Pittsburgh-Lake Erie region. The western Great Lakes have also become important, especially because of the dominance of Chicago as a market center. Canada's most important industrial area is the region around the St. Lawrence Valley, benefiting from its location and the availability of cheap hydroelectric power.

East Asia has become a major industrial region since the second half of the twentieth century by taking advantage of its large labor force. Japan emerged first, followed by South Korea, Taiwan, and China. The latter is now the world's second-largest manufacturer and has the largest labor force.

Key Issue 2—Why Do Industries Have Different Distributions?

A. Key concepts in industrialization

Situation factors involve decisions about industrial location that attempt to minimize transportation costs by considering raw material source(s) as well as the market(s). If the cost of transporting the inputs is greater than the cost of transporting the finished product, the best plant location is nearer to the inputs. Otherwise the best location for the factory will be closer to the consumers.

The North American copper industry is a good example of locating near the raw material source. Copper concentration is a **bulk-reducing industry**; the final product weighs less than the inputs. Two-thirds of U.S. copper is mined in Arizona, so most of the concentration mills and smelters are also in Arizona. Steelmaking is another bulk-reducing industry. Steel was made by the Bessemer process, invented in 1855, which combined iron ore and carbon at very high temperatures using coal to produce steel. By the beginning of the twentieth century most large U.S. steel mills were located near the East and West coasts because iron ore was coming from other countries.

Today the U.S steel industry is located near major markets in minimills. It has become a **footloose industry**, which can locate virtually anywhere because the main input is scrap metal and is available almost everywhere. Today the U.S. steel industry takes advantage of the **agglomeration economies**, or sharing of services with other companies that are available at major markets. The agglomeration of companies can lead to the development of **ancillary activities** that surround and support large-scale industry. **Deglomeration** occurs when a firm leaves an agglomerated region to start in a distant, new place. However, according to Alfred Weber's theory of industrial location or **least-cost theory**, firms will locate where they can minimize transportation and labor costs as well as take advantage of agglomeration economies.

The location of **bulk-gaining industries** is determined largely by the markets because they gain volume or weight during production. Most drink bottling industries are examples of bulk-gaining industries; empty cans or bottles are brought to the bottler, filled, and shipped to consumers.

Single-market manufacturers are specialized, with only one or two customers, such as manufacturers of motor vehicle parts. Obviously they will tend to cluster around their customers. Perishable-product industries such as fresh food and newspapers will usually locate near their markets.

Transportation costs will decline with distance because loading and unloading costs are the greatest. The major modes of transportation are ship, rail, truck, and air. A **break-of-bulk point** is a place where transfer from one mode of transportation to another is possible.

Site factors include labor, land, and capital. **Labor-intensive industries** are those in which the highest percentage of expenses are the cost of employees, such as textile and apparel production. Land, which includes natural resources, is a major site factor. For example, aluminum producers locate near dams to take advantage of hydroelectric power. The availability of capital is critical to the location of high-tech industries, such as those in California's Silicon Valley. The distribution of industries in LDCs is also largely dependent on the ability to borrow money.

Key Issue 3—Where Is Industry Expanding?

B. Growth and diffusion of industrialization
1. The changing roles of energy and technology

C. Contemporary patterns and impacts of industrialization
1. Spatial organization of the world economy
3. Deindustrialization
6. Local development initiatives: government policies

Within regions in MDCs industry has relocated to urban peripheries and rural areas from central city locations. At the interregional level, manufacturing has moved towards the south and west in the United States. Historically industrial growth has been encouraged in the South by government policies to reduce regional disparities. Southern states have enacted **right-to-work laws** that require factories to maintain an "open shop" and prohibit a "closed shop." In a closed shop everyone who works in the factory has to join the union. Thus southern right-to-work laws have made it much more difficult for unions to organize, collect dues, and bargain.

In western Europe government policies and those of the European Union have also encouraged industry to move from wealthier to more impoverished regions. Spain has been a beneficiary of the European Union's Structural Funds for industrial investment.

As industry has declined in MDCs, it has increased in LDCs. In 1980 80% of the world's steel was produced in MDCs. Between 1980 and 2005, MDCs share of steel production declined to 45%, and that of LDCs increased to 55%.

China is the leading new industrial center in the world because of its low labor costs and vast consumer market. Mexico and Brazil are the leading industrial centers in

Latin America, with manufacturing clustered near large cities such as Mexico City and Sao Paulo. Since the 1980s manufacturing in Mexico has moved north to take advantage of the U.S. market, and **maquiladora** plants have been established close to the U.S. border. Maquiladoras, which assemble U.S. parts and ship the finished product back to the United States, have benefited from the **North American Free Trade Agreement (NAFTA)**. NAFTA has eliminated restrictions on the flow of materials and products between the United States and Mexico.

Some central European countries such as Poland, the Czech Republic, and Hungary have received industrial investment since the fall of communism in the early 1990s. They offer less skilled but cheaper labor than western Europe and have locations that are close to major markets.

Key Issue 4—Why Are Location Factors Changing?

B. Growth and diffusion of industrialization
1. The changing roles of energy and technology

C. Contemporary patterns and impacts of industrialization and development
1. Spatial organization of the world economy

The cost of labor is changing the spatial organization of industry around the world. This is particularly true of the textile and apparel industry. In the twentieth century production in the United States moved from the Northeast to the Southeast to take advantage of cheaper wages. More recently the apparel industry is located in Latin America, China, and other Asian countries. Now the United States imports more than 75% of its clothing needs. This is one part of the **new international division of labor**. Industrial jobs are transferring to LDCs largely as a result of transnational corporations' search for low-cost labor. Transnational corporations are **outsourcing**, turning over much of the responsibility for production to independent suppliers.

In some MDCs industry is remaining in traditional regions because of skilled labor and rapid delivery to market. The **Fordist** approach, named for Henry Ford, traditionally assigned each worker a specific task in a mass production industry. **Post-Fordist** production has recently become the norm in MDCs. It is flexible production with skilled workers characterized by teams working together, problem solving through consensus, and factory workers being treated alike regardless of their level.

Just-in-time delivery is the shipment of parts and materials to a factory immediately before they are needed. It avoids the stocking of unnecessary and expensive inventory.

KEY TERMS

Agglomeration economies
Ancillary activities
Break-of-bulk point
Bulk-gaining industry
Bulk-reducing industry
Cottage industry
Deglomeration
Footloose industry
Fordist
Industrial Revolution
Just-in-time delivery
Labor-intensive industry

Least-cost theory
Maquiladora
New international division of labor
North American Free Trade Agreement
    (NAFTA)
Outsourcing
Post-Fordist
Right-to-work-laws
Site factors
Situation factors
Textile

CHAPTER 12: SERVICES

In MDCs most workers are employed in the tertiary sector of the economy, which is the provision of goods and services. There is a close relationship between services and settlements; most services are clustered in settlements. Beyond that they are also clustered in MDCs because that is where people are more likely to be able to buy services, rather than LDCs. Within MDCs business services locate in large settlements that are also the key markets. This chapter concludes by addressing why services cluster downtown.

Key Issue 1—Where Did Services Originate?

VII. Cities and Urban Land Use

C. Functional character of contemporary cities
1. Changing employment mix

In North America, three-quarters of employees work in the service sector. There are three types of services: consumer services, business services, and public services.

Consumer services provide services to individual consumers and include retail services and personal services. Retail services include about 11% of all jobs in the United States and provide goods for sale to consumers. Other consumer services include education services, health services, and leisure and hospitality services.

Business services help other businesses and include financial services, professional services, transportation, communication, and utilities services; they diffuse and distribute services.

Public services, which include governmental services at various levels, provide security and protection for citizens and businesses.

United States employment in the service sector has increased as employment in primary and secondary sector activities has declined during the twentieth century. Employment has increased most rapidly in personal and producer services. Public services have increased at the slowest rate.

V. Agriculture and Rural Land Use

C. Rural land use and settlement patterns
2. Settlement patterns associated with major agricultural types

A large percentage of the world's population still practice agriculture and live in rural settlements. In **clustered rural settlements**, families live to close to one another and fields surround houses and farm buildings. In **dispersed rural settlements**, farmers live on individual farms and are more isolated from their neighbors.

Circular rural settlements consist of a central open space surrounded by buildings. The medieval German *Gewandorf* settlements and East African Masai villages are examples of circular settlements. Linear rural settlements are clustered along transportation like roads or rivers. In North America most linear settlements can be traced to the original French *longlot* or *seigneurial* pattern.

Dispersed rural settlements are more associated with more recent agricultural settlements in the developed world. In some European countries clustered patterns were converted to dispersed settlements. The rural **enclosure movement** that accompanied the Industrial Revolution in Britain is a good example of this transition. It provided greater efficiency in an agricultural world that relied on fewer farmers.

Key Issue 2—Why Are Consumer Services Distributed in a Regular Pattern?

VII. Cities and Urban Land Use

B. Origin and evolution of cities
4. Models of urban systems

Consumer services are generally provided in a regular pattern based on size of settlements, with larger settlements offering more than smaller ones.

Central Place Theory examines the relationship between settlements of different sizes, especially their ability to provide various goods and services. It was developed by Walter Christaller in the 1930s and was based on his studies of settlement patterns in southern Germany. A service will have a **market area** or **hinterland** of potential customers. Each urban settlement will have a market area, assuming that people will get services from the nearest settlement. The **range** is the maximum distance that people are willing to travel for a service, and the **threshold** is the minimum number of people needed to support a service. Retailers and other service providers will use these concepts to analyze the potential market area.

The **gravity model** predicts that the best location for a service is directly related to the number of people in the area and inversely related to the distance that people must travel for it. A place with more people will have more potential customers, and people who are further away from a service are less likely to use it.

Services and settlements are hierarchical, and larger settlements will provide consumer services that have larger thresholds, ranges, and market areas than smaller settlements. Central place theory shows market areas in MDCs as a series of hexagons of various sizes. Christaller identifies four different levels of market area and seven different settlement sizes. Since this is a theory he made certain assumptions that may or may not be true in reality, such as equal ease of transportation in all directions, and that people would always get a service from the nearest available market.

Geographers have observed that, in many MDCs, there is sometimes a regular hierarchy of settlements from largest to smallest. This is the **rank size rule**, where a country's *n*th-largest settlement is 1/*n*th the population of the largest settlement. So the second largest city would be half the size of the largest. The hierarchy of towns and cities in the United States follows the rank size rule fairly well, which shows that goods and services are provided to consumers at many levels throughout the country. Many LDCs as well as some European countries follow the **primate city rule** rather than the rank size rule. A **primate city** is much larger and more important than any other city in that country. This is true of Buenos Aires, Argentina, and Copenhagen, Denmark.

In settlements at the lower end of the central place hierarchy, **periodic markets** may be set up. These are collections of individual vendors who offer goods and services in a specific location one of two times a week. They exist all over the globe.

Key Issue 3—Who Do Business Services Locate in Large Settlements?

VII. Cities and Urban Land Use

B. Origin and evolution of cities
3. Global cities and megacities

There have been major urban settlements in different parts of the world since ancient times, including Mesopotamia, Greece, and Rome. In ancient Greece **city-states** such as Athens and Sparta emerged. These included the city and surrounding countryside or hinterland. Cities in the Roman world, especially Rome, were important centers of administration, trade, culture, and a host of other services. Urbanization declined with the fall of Rome and didn't reemerge until the eleventh century. From the time of the fall of Rome until the Industrial Revolution the largest cities in the world were in Asia.

Modern world cities offer business services, especially financial services. They also have retail services with huge market areas, such as leisure and cultural services of national importance. London presents more plays than the rest of Britain combined. World cities are also centers of national and international power. New York is the headquarters of the United Nations, and Brussels is one of the headquarter cities of the European Union.

Four levels of cities have been identified by geographers. These are world cities, regional command and control centers, specialized producer-service centers, and dependent centers. London, New York, and Tokyo are at the top of the hierarchy of world cities. They are unique in that they all have important international stock exchanges. There are also second and third tier world cities.

C. Functional character of contemporary cities
1. Changing employment mix

Command and control centers contain the headquarters of large corporations, and concentrations of a variety of business services. There are regional centers like Atlanta and Boston, and subregional centers such as Charlotte and Des Moines.

Specialized producer-service centers have management and research and development activities associated with specific industries. Detroit is a specialized producer-service center specializing in motor vehicles.

As the term suggests, dependent centers depend on decisions made in world cities for their economic well-being. They provide relatively unskilled jobs. San Diego is an industrial and military dependent center.

Basic industries are exported mainly to consumers outside a settlement and constitute that community's **economic base**. These industries employ a large percentage of a community's workforce. **Nonbasic industries** are usually consumed within that community. Basic industries are vital to the economic health of a settlement. The concept of basic industries originally referred to the secondary sector of the economy, such as manufacturing but in a **postindustrial society** such as the United States, they are now more likely to be in the service sector of the economy.

Key Issue 4—Why Do Services Cluster Downtown?

VII. Cities and Urban Land Use

C. Functional character of contemporary cities
1. Changing employment mix

The **central business district (CBD)** is the center of a city where services have traditionally clustered. Specifically three types of retail services have concentrated in the center because they require accessibility. These include services with a high threshold, those with a long range, and those that serve people who work in the center. A large department store is a service with a high threshold. Retail services with a high range are specialized shops that are patronized infrequently. Both of these types of services have moved in large numbers to suburban locations in recent years. Services that cater to people working in the CBD have remained in this location and have actually expanded, especially where CBDs have been revitalized. Business services such as advertising and banking have also remained clustered in the CBD.

Manufacturing has declined in MDCs. Industries that have not closed have moved their operations to the suburbs where they can take advantage of cheaper land. Residents have also moved away from CBDs. Pull factors have lured them to the suburbs; the crime and poverty of central cities have acted as a push factor.

D. Built environment and social space
4. Urban planning and design

Land costs in the CBD are very high because of competition for accessibility. Thus land use is more intensive in the CBD and the built character is more vertical than other parts of urban areas, both above and belowground. Infrastructure, including transportation and utilities, typically runs underground. Skyscrapers give the central city its distinctive image. Washington, D.C., is the only large U.S. CBD that does not have skyscrapers because no building is allowed to be higher than the U.S. Capitol dome. European CBDs are visibly very different because they have tried to preserve their historic cores by limiting high-rise buildings.

C. Functional character of contemporary cities
1. Changing employment mix

North American suburbs are no longer just areas of residential growth. Businesses have moved to the suburbs. Retailing has become concentrated in suburban malls. Factories and offices have also moved to suburbia. If they don't require face-to-face contact they can take advantage of the lower rents in the suburbs.

KEY TERMS

Basic industries
Business services
Central business district (CBD)
Central place theory
City-state
Clustered rural settlement
Consumer services
Dispersed rural settlement
Economic base
Enclosure movement
Gravity model
Hinterland

Market area
Nonbasic industries
Periodic markets
Postindustrial society
Primate city
Primate city rule
Public services
Range
Service
Settlement
Threshold

CHAPTER 13: URBAN PATTERNS

Urban geographers are concerned with the global distribution of urban settlements as well as the distribution of people and activities within urban areas. The chapter examines models that have been developed to help explain the internal structure of urban areas in the North America and elsewhere. The distinctive problems of inner cities and suburbs are also considered.

Key Issue 1—Where Have Urban Areas Grown?

VII. Cities and Urban Land Use

A. Definitions of urbanism

The first cities emerged thousands of years ago but, as recently as 1800, only three percent of the world's population lived in cities. Today nearly half of the world's people live in cities. About three-quarters of people living in MDCs live in urban areas compared to about two-fifths in LDCs, although urbanization in Latin America is comparable to MDCs. **Urban geography** deals with all aspects of cities, including their historical development, spatial development, interaction with surrounding regions, and role in the world economic system. **Urbanization** is the process by which the population of cities grows, both in *numbers* and *percentage*.

In the 1930s Louis Wirth, an urban geographer, defined a **city** as a permanent settlement that has a large size, high population density, and socially heterogeneous people. Urban settlements today can be physically defined by legal boundary, as continuously built-up area, and as a functional area.

B. Origin and evolution of cities
1. Historical patterns of urbanization
2. Rural-urban migration and urban growth

Urbanism dates back almost to the time of sedentary agriculture but developed very slowly. In Europe Athens and Rome were important urban areas in the ancient world, but urban life did not thrive in the early Middle Ages. Cities developed in Asia and the Americas at this time. The great European cities, such as Madrid, Prague, Vienna, and Amsterdam, emerged during the 1400s. The Spanish developed colonial cities in the Americas during the 1500s. It was during the eighteenth century in association with the Industrial Revolution that urbanism really took off on a global scale.

In MDCs a large percentage of people living in urban areas is one measure of a country's level of development. Urbanization over the last 200 years in MDCs is a consequence of rural to urban migration to work in factories and services. LDCs have also experienced more recent rural to urban migration in search of economic activities in cities. Unfortunately urban jobs are much less available in LDCs.

MDCs have higher percentages of urban dwellers, but LDCs have larger numbers of people living in urban areas. Seven of the ten most populous cities, including Mexico City, Sao Paulo, and Seoul. These are **megacities** and are characterized by chaotic growth, pollution, and poverty. This is a big change from 100 years ago when 9 of the top 10 urban areas were located in MDCs.

D. Built environment and social space
3. Political organization of urban areas

Virtually all countries have a political system that recognizes cities as legal entities with fixed boundaries. In the United States a city that is surrounded by suburbs is sometimes called a **central city**. The central city and surrounding suburbs are together called an **urbanized area**.

The U.S. Census Bureau defines the functional areas of cities for political and economic purposes. A **Metropolitan Statistical Area (MSA)** includes a central city of at least 50,000 with high density adjacent counties where the majority of inhabitants work in non-agricultural jobs. The census has also designated smaller urban areas as **micropolitan statistical areas**. These include an urbanized area of between 10,000 and 50,000 inhabitants and adjacent counties tied to the city. A **Consolidated Metropolitan Statistical Area (CMSA)** consists of two adjacent MSAs with overlapping commuter patterns such as the Washington-Baltimore CMSA. Within a CMSA, an MSA that exceeds one million people may be classified as a **Primary Metropolitan Statistical Area (PMSA)**. The metropolitan areas of the northeastern United States now form one continuous urban complex or **megalopolis** (from the Greek word meaning great city).

Key Issue 2—Where Are People Distributed within Urban Areas?

D. Built environment and social space
1. Comparative models of internal city structure

Three different models were developed in Chicago to help explain the internal spatial organization of the urban environment. The **concentric zone model** was developed in 1923 by Burgess, and describes cities that have concentric rings of urban land use emanating outward from a core or **central business district (CBD)**. The rings each contain different kinds of urban land use and residences become more high class further away from the CBD.

The **sector model** was developed in 1939 by Hoyt, who saw the city developing as a series of sectors rather than rings. They believed that cities have numerous **nodes** of business and other urban land uses rather than one central core. The sectors often followed transportation lines. Hoyt and Burgess both claimed that social patterns in Chicago supported their model.

The **multiple nuclei model** was developed by Harris and Ullman in 1945. They believed that cities lack one central core but instead have numerous **nodes** of business and cultural activities. Although dated, these models help geographers to understand where different people live in an urban area and why they live there. Cities in MDCs as well as LDCs exhibit characteristics of these models, but no one city matches any model perfectly.

In order to apply these models to reality, accurate data needs to be available. In the United States that information is available from the U.S. Census Bureau, which has divided urban areas into **census tracts**, which are essentially urban neighborhoods.

These three models were developed to describe the spatial distribution of social classes in the urban United States. However, they can also be applied to urbanization outside North America. In European cities wealthier people tend to live closer to the CBD, and there is more suburban poverty. European cities are also much older and still retain their medieval city center.

Islamic cities, such as Mecca, were laid out surrounding a religious core. They have mosques and a bazaar or marketplace at their center with walls guarding the perimeter. In the outer rings there were secular businesses and quarters laid out for Jews (**ghetto**) and foreigners. Some features of these cities were adaptations to the hot and dry physical environment.

In Asia, Africa, and Latin America cities combine elements of native culture, colonial rule, religion, industry, and poverty. Griffin and Ford developed a model of a **Latin American city** which shows the wealthy living close to the CBD. Industrial sectors radiate out from the CBD, and the poorest live on the urban fringe in **squatter settlements**. The latter are known by a variety of names such as *barrios*, *barriadas*, and *favelas* in Latin America, *bidonvilles* in North Africa, and *bustees* in India.

Key Issue 3—Why Do Inner Cities Have Distinctive Problems?

C. Functional character of contemporary cities
2. Changing demographic and social structures

D. Built environment and social space
2. Transportation and infrastructure
4. Urban planning and design
5. Patterns of race, ethnicity, gender, and class
6. Uneven development, ghettoization, and gentrification

Inner cities in the United States have a multitude of physical, social, and economic problems. One of the major physical problems is **filtering**, which is when houses are subdivided and occupied by successive waves of lower-income people. It can lead to total abandonment. As a result of filtering, inner-city neighborhoods have rapidly declining populations. **Redlining** is when banks draw lines on a map to identify areas where they will refuse to loan money, although the Community Reinvestment Act has essentially made this illegal.

Governments at various levels have put together grants to help the revitalization of inner-city neighborhoods. This process is called **urban renewal**. Substandard inner-city housing has been demolished and replaced with **public housing** for low-income people. Many of the public high-rise projects built during the 1950s and 1960s have since been demolished because they were considered unsafe. More recently the trend has been to renovate deteriorating inner-city houses so that they will appeal to middle-class people. This process is known as **gentrification**.

There are numerous inner-city social problems, too. Many of the residents are considered an **underclass** because they are trapped in a cycle of economic and social problems. Many lack the necessary job skills for even the most basic jobs, and there are more than three million homeless in the United States today. This culture of poverty leads to various crimes, including drug use, gangs, and other criminal activities.

Most inner-city residents cannot pay the taxes that are necessary to provide the necessary public services. Federal government contributions have helped, but these have declined substantially since the 1980s. State governments have increased financial assistance to cities. Economic problems have been made worse because cities have not been able to annex adjacent land. **Annexation** is the process of legally adding land area to a city. In the United States most surrounding suburban lands have their own jurisdictions and want to remain legally independent of the central city.

Key Issue 4—Why Do Suburbs Have Distinctive Problems?

D. Built environment and social space
1. Comparative models of internal city structure
7. Impacts of suburbanization and edge cities

North American cities are increasingly following a structure that Harris calls the **peripheral model**. The peripheral model consists of an inner city surrounded by growing suburbs that combine residential and business areas and are tied together by a beltway or ring road. Nodes of business and consumer services called **edge cities** have developed around the beltway. Edge cities have grown from suburbs that were originally primarily residential.

In North American urban areas, the further one gets from the center of the city, there will be a decline in the density at which people live. This is called the **density gradient**. The number of houses per unit area of land will decline with distance from the center city. In North American and European cities in recent years, the density gradient has leveled out as more people have moved to the suburbs. **Suburban sprawl** has increased at the expense of agricultural land, and it results in the need for costly infrastructure. Several British cities are surrounded by **greenbelts**, or rings of open space, to prevent suburban sprawl. **Zoning ordinances**, which prevent the mixing of land uses, have resulted in segregated residential suburbs. Residents are separated from industrial and service activities, and poorer residents are excluded because of the cost, size, or location of housing.

2. Transportation and infrastructure

Urban sprawl has resulted in an increased dependence on transportation, especially motor vehicles in the United States. Public transportation is much more important in most European and Japanese cities. Public transportation in the form of rapid transit is becoming more common in U.S. cities, although it is still not recognized as a key utility that needs to be subsidized.

3. Political organization of urban areas

Many urban regional problems cannot be easily solved because of the fragmentation of local government. There are 1,400 local governments in the New York area alone, and 20,000 throughout the United States. Most U.S. metropolitan areas have a **council of government**, consisting of representatives of the various local governments, that can do some planning for the entire area. There are two kinds of metropolitan-wide governments. A **federation system** of government combines the various municipalities of a metropolitan area into a single government. Toronto, Ontario, has a federation system. Some U.S. cities have consolidated city and county governments. Indianapolis and Miami are both examples of **consolidations**.

Several U.S. states are passing legislation and regulations called **smart growth**; it limits suburban sprawl and preserves farmland on the urban periphery. Maryland has done an especially good job in this area.

KEY TERMS

Annexation
Central Business District (CBD)
Central city
Census tract
City
Concentric zone model
Consolidated Metropolitan Statistical
    Area (CMSA)
Consolidations
Council of government
Density gradient
Edge city
Federations
Filtering
Gentrification
Ghetto
Greenbelt
Islamic city

Latin American city
Megacity
Megalopolis
Metropolitan Statistical Area (MSA)
Micropolitan statistical area
Multiple nuclei model
Nodes
Peripheral model
Primary Metropolitan Statistical Area
    (PMSA)
Public housing
Redlining
Sector model
Smart growth
Sprawl
Squatter settlements
Underclass
Urban geography

Urbanization
Urbanized area

Urban renewal
Zoning ordinance

CHAPTER 14: RESOURCE ISSUES

A **resource** is a substance in the environment that is useful as well as feasible to access. Resources include water, soil, plants, animals, and minerals. This chapter deals with the two major misuses of resources, the depletion of scarce resources for energy production and the destruction of resources through pollution.

Key Issue 1—Why Are Resources Being Depleted?

VI. Industrialization and Economic Development

B. Growth and diffusion of industrialization
1. The changing roles of energy and technology

Animate power is supplied by humans and animals. Since the Industrial Revolution there has been a tremendous increase in **inanimate power**, which is generated by machines. Three **fossil fuels**, oil, natural gas, and coal, provide five-sixths of the world's energy. In some LDCs **biomass fuel**, such as wood, plant material, and animal waste, is still the major source of fuel.

Fossil fuels are examples of **nonrenewable energy**. Remaining supplies are **proven reserves** and **potential reserves**. The world's proven reserves of natural gas will last for about 60 years, which is less than petroleum reserves and much less than coal reserves. New technology can make potential reserves a reality but extraction is now much harder. New fields may yet be discovered, and unconventional sources may be developed.

Fossil fuels are unevenly distributed around the globe. China extracts 40% of the world's total, and the United States extracts 20%. Australia, India, Russia, and South Africa also all have major reserves. Saudi Arabia, Iran, Iraq, Kuwait, and the United Arab Emirates, all of which are members of the **Organization of Petroleum Exporting Countries (OPEC)**, have 60 % of the world's oil reserves. Russia and the United States each account for one-fourth of world natural gas production. A few LDCs in Africa, Asia, and Latin America have extensive reserves of one or more fossil fuels, but most have little. MDCs currently consume about three-quarters of the world's energy, although LDCs, especially China, are beginning to consume more as they become more developed.

Nuclear power is becoming an increasing energy source, and it now supplies about one-sixth of the world's electricity. The world's leading generators of nuclear power are the United States, France, and Japan. Problems associated with nuclear power include potential accidents, **radioactive waste**, generation of plutonium, a limited uranium supply, geographic distribution, and cost.

Minerals are plentiful on the Earth's surface and are potential resources if people can find a use for them. Minerals are either metallic or nonmetallic. Nonmetallic metals include various stones and sand, as well as nitrogen, phosphorus and other sources of fertilizer. Metallic minerals are ferrous, derived from iron, or **nonferrous** of which the most abundant is aluminum.

Key Issue 2—Why Are Resources Being Polluted?

VI. Industrialization and Economic Development

C. Contemporary patterns and impacts of industrialization and development
4. Pollution, health, and quality of life

Air, water, and land remove and disperse waste, but **pollution** will occur when more waste is added than a resource can accommodate. **Air pollution** is a concentration of trace substances at a greater level than occurs in average air. The burning of fossil fuels generates most air pollution. Air pollution may contribute to global warming because of the **greenhouse effect**, which is when carbon dioxide traps some of the radiation emitted by the Earth's surface. The **ozone** layer of the Earth's atmosphere absorbs dangerous ultraviolet (UV) rays from the Sun but is threatened by pollutants called **chlorofluorocarbons (CFCs).**

Pollution in the atmosphere may return to the Earth's surface as **acid precipitation**, which damages lakes and agricultural land in regions of heavy industrial development. Urban air pollution consists of carbon monoxide, hydrocarbons, and particulates. This is a serious problem in urban areas such as Denver and Santiago, Chile, where the mountains help to trap the gases and produce a temperature inversion.

Most water pollution is generated by water-using industries, municipal sewage, and agriculture. Polluted water can harm aquatic plants and animals. It also causes waterborne diseases such as cholera, typhoid, and dysentery, especially in LDCs that suffer from poor sanitation and untreated water.

Paper products constitute the largest percentage of solid waste in the United States. Most of this waste is disposed in **sanitary landfills**. The number of landfills in the United States has declined by three-fourths since 1990; there are now a smaller number of larger regional landfills. Incineration reduces the bulk of trash by about three-fourths, but burning release toxins into the air. The disposal of hazardous waste is especially difficult. Hazardous waste sites, such as Love Canal, near Niagara Falls, New York, have leaked and caused health problems.

Key Issue 3—Why Are Resources Reusable?

VI. Industrialization and Economic Development

B. Growth and diffusion of industrialization
1. The changing roles of energy and technology

C. Contemporary patterns and impacts of industrialization and development
5. Industrialization, environmental change, and sustainability

The leading **renewable resources** are biomass and hydroelectric power. Geothermal and wind power are also becoming important. Wood and plants are important forms of biomass that are renewable resources if they are carefully harvested. The energy of moving water has been used to generate **hydroelectric power**, which is the second-most important source of electricity after coal, supplying about one-fourth of the world's demand. The biggest drawback with hydroelectric power is that it is often generated by the building of dams that can cause serious environmental damage. **Geothermal energy** is generated from hot water or steam in volcanic areas, especially Iceland.

Solar energy is free and **ubiquitous**, and thus potentially the most important renewable resource. It can be harnessed either through passive or active means. **Passive solar energy systems** capture solar energy without any special devices, whereas **active solar energy systems** collect solar energy and convert it to heat energy or electricity. **Recycling** is the separation, collection, processing, and reuse of unwanted material. Recycling has increased in the United States from 7% of all solid waste in 1970 to about 32% in 2005. Recycled products are picked up, processed, and manufactured into marketable products

Key Issue 4—Why Can Resources Be Conserved?

VI. Industrialization and Economic Development

C. Contemporary patterns and impacts of industrialization and development
5. Industrialization, environmental change, and sustainability

According to the United Nations, **sustainable development** is "development that meets the needs of the present without compromising the ability of future generations to meet their own needs." **Preservation** is the maintenance of resources in their present condition, whereas **conservation** is the sustainable use and management of natural resources. Sustainable development advocates the limited use of renewable resources so that the environment can supply them indefinitely. Some critics, such as the World Wildlife Fund, argue that the world surpassed its sustainable level around 1980.

Closely related to sustainable development is **biodiversity**, which refers to the variety of plant and animal species across the Earth's surface or in a specific place. When biodiversity is protected, sustainable development is promoted. More than one-half of the Earth's species are located in tropical forests, and the main cause of high rates of species extinction is rapid deforestation.

KEY TERMS

Acid precipitation
Active solar energy systems
Air pollution
Animate power
Biodiversity
Biomass fuel
Chlorofluorocarbon (CFC)
Conservation
Ferrous
Fossil fuels
Geothermal energy
Greenhouse effect
Hydroelectric power
Inanimate power
Nonferrous
Nonrenewable energy

Organization of Petroleum Exporting
    Countries (OPEC)
Ozone
Passive solar energy systems
Pollution
Potential reserve
Preservation
Proven reserve
Radioactive waste
Recycling
Renewable energy
Resource
Sanitary landfill
Sustainable development
Ubiquitous energy/resources

Activities

Activity One—Geography: Its Nature and Perspectives

Geographers study the relationship between humans and the environment. When analyzing the spatial distributions of human settlements, they are looking for a global connection or pattern to understand this relationship. Think about the two theories of where humans live on Earth—possibilism and environmental determinism—to answer the following questions.

Look at the following map series: 1-14 (climate regions), 2-2 (World Population), 2-3 (Ecumene), 2-4 (Arithmetic Density), and 2-5 (Physiological Density).

1. Is there a relationship between map 1-14 and 2-2?
2. Now compare 1-14 and 2-3 for a historical look at human settlements. Is there a relationship between these maps?
3. Compare 1-14 with 2-4; is there a relationship between population density and climate?
4. Now compare 1-14 to 2-5; can you see a relationship there?
5. If you glance at all map sets, what conclusion can you draw about the relationship between the environment and spatial patterns of settlement?
6. With this evidence, does one theory hold true?

Possible Answers:

1. It appears that areas that are most populated are located in regions with humid tropical, semiarid, humid subtropical, and humid continental climates. There is definitely a correlation between the maps in the subarctic, ice cap, and tundra climates, where people do not live.

2. Intensive settlement throughout time has been located near coastlines, and if rivers were present on these maps, you would notice that the settlement pattern is also near them.

3. The relationship between the arithmetic density map and the climate map does not seem to hold true compared to the choropleth dot map, 2-2. The difference in this map projection is that on 2-4 it is obvious that in places such as India with a high arithmetic density, if people were distributed uniformly across the landscape, people would be living in desert climates as well. The better comparison for where people live would be in comparing the first map sets, which shows the location of the majority of people.

4. Physiological density is the number of people per unit area of arable land, so when we look at climate maps to compare, it appears that there is a relationship between the desert and the physiological density. As you think about it that makes sense. In the desert, one area of farmland would need to feed more people, therefore the density would be higher. So on this map; we see a direct correlation to climate regions.

5. Humans will live where the climate is fairly mild and where they have easy access to the coast and fresh water. Landlocked countries on all of these map sets show that they

are less likely to have large human settlements, as are areas with harsh climates. It is also obvious from this comparison that areas with large populations are not evenly distributed, even within a country (look at India and China). The global commonalities that affect where people live are that two-thirds of the world lives within 300 miles of the ocean, in low-lying areas with fertile soil and temperate climates, in the Northern Hemisphere between 10–55 degrees latitude.

6. Environmental determinism (Humboldt and Ritter) explains the relationship between the physical environment and human actions. Possibilism says that the physical environment may limit some human actions but that people have the ability to adjust to their environment, so in fact both theories might hold true. However, if you look only at the maps, Humboldt and Ritter's theory would hold because according to the maps, people are living in environments that are conducive to human actions (i.e., farming). It would be difficult to prove, via the maps, possibilism, as there is not evidence supporting people living in extreme conditions, such as the Arctic.

Activity Two—Population

When looking at population issues, geographers are interested in the question, "Is the world overpopulated?" As we study this issue, we look at many different criteria to find the answer.

1.   Define in your own words the term "overpopulation." Do you think the world is overpopulated? Why? Why not? Would Malthus agree with you? What about Esther Boserup?

2.   Define the following terms: crude birthrate, crude death rate, rate of natural increase, total fertility rate, age cohort, and dependency ratio.

3.   Go on the Internet to the site http://www.census.gov/ipc/www/idbpyr.html and analyze population pyramids for the following countries: China, India, Indonesia, and France. Create a table which compares and contrasts these pyramids.

4.   What conclusions/predictions can you make about population growth in the four populated regions of the Earth that you obtained population pyramids for?

Possible Answers:

1.   Overpopulation is the relationship between the total number of people on Earth and the availability of resources. Many population theorists, like Malthus, would say that because population grows exponentially and food supply grows arithmetically, eventually we will not be able to feed our people. Unlike Malthus, Esther Boserup believed that humans are unique creatures, who will be able, through technological advances in agriculture, to produce enough food to feed the masses.

2.   Crude birthrate is the # of live persons per 1,000.

Crude death rate is the # of deaths per 1,000.

Total fertility rate is the # of women between the ages of 15–49.

Rate of natural increase is the percentage by which population grows each year.

Age cohort is the breakdown of a population by age, (i.e., 0–4 years old would be a cohort).

Dependency ratio is the number of young and old people in a population who are not in the workforce.

3.

COUNTRY	SIMILARITIES	DIFFERENCES
CHINA	•Shaped like France •Evidence to support a population explosion around 1970 due to bulge in age cohort 30-35 in 2000, in France, too •Women will outlive men •Population continues to be high because of the amount of people who were present when the government imposed population policies. It will take until 2050 to see an actual decline in the total population.	•Extremely high total population compared to Indonesia and France •India and Indonesia do not appear to have experienced a population explosion in any cohort (no baby boom)
INDIA	•India and Indonesia are both bell shaped, which supports a continuing population growth •The population will continue to growth, as in Indonesia, and will have fewer older people to support the young	•Unlike France and China, it does not appear that India's rate of natural increase is going to slow down in the next 50 years •Similarly, India will continue to have a large majority of their population young and within the total fertility rate
INDONESIA	•Like India, the population pyramids are bell shaped •Population is predicted to continue to grow for the next 50 years	•Unlike India or China, Indonesia's overall population is quite a bit smaller •Indonesia's population will begin to age in the next 50 years and the age cohorts age 65 will see great increases
FRANCE	•Population pyramids for France are similar to China, in that they are in a column shape •Like China, France appears to have had a population explosion (baby boom) in the 1970s	•France has a low total population compared to all three other countries •By 2050 France will be the only country with people living longer than 100 years

4.   As population continues to stabilize in places like China and India, they will still experience population stresses, because of the total number of people in their populations. India and Indonesia will have a large number of children who will need to be taken care of (i.e., health care, education). France, on the other hand, will lower their youth and will increase their elderly. Who will take care of the very old? Who will pay into the national health care system, since there are fewer workers?

Remember that many people can argue that the world is overpopulated and others may argue that it is not, the theme that you should always look for is the spatial distribution of people on Earth. It can be possible that certain regions are overpopulated and cannot provide necessary resources for their people.

Activity Three—Cultural Patterns and Processes

Geographers are interested in the spatial distribution of culture. Remember that culture is like luggage, people carry it with them wherever they go (relocation diffusion). In this activity you are asked to identify influences from other parts of the world and other cultures that have become part of your culture group.

1. List the types of leisure activities people in your town are involved with.
2. What type of food is dominant in your cultural group?
3. What is the predominant type of housing present?
4. What language do most people speak? Are other languages spoken?
5. What religion dominates your cultural landscape?
6. What is the main ethnic group present in your town? Are others present? How can you tell?

By analyzing your answers to these questions, is there an "American Culture," or are we a melting pot of cultures?

Possible Answers (of course these will vary according to your geographic location):

1. In my town, most leisure activities revolve around sports. People go to watch our profession sports teams, basketball, soccer, baseball, lacrosse, and football. They also participate in many sports, including water and snow skiing. Our cultural landscape reflects this, with the many sporting venues for professional athletes.
2. I would say there are many types of food present. Our city has many ethnic restaurants that reflect the many different types of people that live here. Overall, most people like steak and potatoes or McDonalds.
3. All of the housing looks the same in the suburbs, downtown; houses are very old and made of bricks.
4. Most people speak English as their predominant language; however, other languages such as Spanish can be heard.
5. Christianity is the main religion. Many different denominations are present. You can see many types of churches as you drive down a main road; Protestant, Catholic, even Eastern Orthodox.
6. Most people living here are white. I know that there are also areas with different ethnic groups; Hispanic, Vietnamese, and Ethiopian all are present. I can tell this from the signs on buildings and streets (toponyms). Also the types of food and other services available reflect this.

It seems that there is an "American Culture" that is made up of blue jeans, fast cars, and fast foods; and part of that culture has embedded within it a melting pot from all corners of the world.

Activity Four—Political Organization of Space

In this unit, the focus has been on how boundaries are formed in the world. You looked at historical divisions with colonial boundaries being drawn that did not mesh with ethnic boundaries. In our contemporary world, since the fall of the Soviet Union and end of the cold war, boundaries continue to be redefined. One of the ever present situations in Europe, as you have read, is the expansion of the European Union into Eastern Bloc countries.

This activity deals with the European Union granting Turkey membership. This membership has come with a barrage of criticism. If you were a voting member of the European Union, how would you vote?

1.   Go to the website http://en.wikipedia.org/wiki/European_Union.
2.   Complete the following chart regarding European Union membership.

Member nations	
Governmental leaders	
Institutions and their geographic locations	
Candidate countries	

3.   Does Turkey meet the criteria for joining? If so, what other issues come up when you were investigating its entrance into the EU?

4.   How would you vote and why?

Possible Answers:
1.   Website access

2.

Member Nations	Belgium, France, West Germany, Italy, Luxembourg, Netherlands (1957), Denmark, Ireland, United Kingdom (1973), Greece (1981), Portugal, Spain (1986), East Germany after reunification (1990), Austria, Finland, Sweden (1995), Cyprus, Czech Republic, Estonia, Hungary, Latvia, Lithuania, Malta, Poland, Slovakia, Slovenia (2004), Bulgaria, and Romania (2007)
Governmental leaders	EU Summit—Angela Merkel/Germany Council—Frank-Walter Steinmeier Commission—Jose Manuel Barroso Parliament—Hans-Gert Pottering
Institutions and their geographic locations	European Commission: Brussels, Belgium European Parliament: Strasbourg, Germany European Court of Justice: Luxembourg European Central Bank: Frankfurt, Germany
Candidate countries	Turkey, Croatia, Albania, Bosnia and Herzegovina, Montenegro, and Serbia

3.   Turkey might eventually be able to meet the criteria, if they do the economic and social reforms that the European Union charter calls for. However, significant issues will hamper their entry: the Cyprus dispute, issues about the Armenia Holocaust, possibly the fact that they have a Muslim majority and last, one of geography—is Turkey entirely in Europe? The original charter does not specify strict geographic criteria, but the EU Parliament continues to bring up the issue that Turkey lies both in Europe and Asia, so political geography comes into play. It is quite clear from all evidence that they will not be joining any time soon.

4.   ANSWERS WILL VARY…. Possible answer, yes, I would vote for them to join because as you look at the natural of a supranational organization like the European Union, the formation was to promote economic stability in the region and now possibly peace and security. If a country such as Turkey is allowed to join, it will be able, due to its geographic location, to help the EU obtain these goals.

Activity Five—Agricultural and Rural Land Use

As you learned in this unit, geographers try to find patterns across the landscape. If you've ever flown in an airplane, then you know that agricultural practices are quite evident on the landscape. In this activity, you will try to determine where the "typical" farmer in the world might be located and what type of agriculture practices they would use.

1.   Look at FIGURE 10-5 in your book. This map set compares climate regions with distinctive types of agricultural practices around the world. Based on your knowledge of agriculture, answer the following questions:
        A.   What type of farming occurs in dry regions of the world?
        B.   What type of farming is practiced in India?
        C.   What about China?
        D.   What is the predominant type of farming found in the western part of the United States?
        E.   What about the area east of the Mississippi River?
        F.   What type of farming is practiced in western Europe?
        G.   What is the difference between farming in India and China with farming in the United States and western Europe?
2.   Now look at FIGURE 2-2 (World Population).
        A.   Where are the most populated regions in the world?
        B.   What type of farming is practiced there?
3.   Based on your analysis, what type of agricultural activity would the "typical" farmer be participating in and where would this farmer be located?

Possible Answers:

1.   A.   Dry regions have little or no agriculture and pastoral nomadism. There are, however, little pockets of commercial gardening present.
        B.   Indians practice intensive subsistence, wet rice dominant, intensive subsistence, wet rice not dominant, shifting cultivation, and plantation.
        C.   The Chinese are similar to the Indians; however large portions of western Chinese practice pastoral nomadism.
        D.   Livestock ranching and some grain production.
        E.   East of the Mississippi River, the United States practices dairy farming, mixed crop, and livestock and grain production.
        F.   Western European nations practice Mediterranean agriculture, dairy, mixed crop, and livestock agriculture.
        G.   India and China practice subsistence agriculture, whereas the United States and western Europe practice commercial agriculture.
2.   A.   The most populated regions are in India and Southeast Asia.
        B.   The type of farming is subsistence agriculture.
3.   The "typical farmer" would be found in South Asia and would practice subsistence agriculture.

Activity Six—Industrialization and Economic Development

When geographers are looking at the issue of development, they undoubtedly notice the spatial distribution of industrialized nations as well as those nations living in extreme poverty. Occasionally, when looking at the world in this way, we see the world aligned in two groups: the haves versus have-nots.

1. Look at the map on More or Less Developed regions of the world, FIGURE 9-8. This line is usually referred to as the Brandt Line, after Willy Brandt who wrote a report, "The North/South Divide."

2. Now look at FIGURE 9-1 (Human Development Index Map) and FIGURE 9-2 (Gross Domestic Product Map). Is there any correlation between FIGURE 9-8 and these maps? What can you conclude about the living standards of people who live above the line and below?

Possible Answers:

1. Access to the map.
2. The FIGURE 9-1 seems to be perfectly correlated with FIGURE 9-8. When I look at FIGURE 9-2, the correlation becomes even clearer. Regions to the north of the line have a high Human Development Index and higher per capita Gross Domestic Product than those to the South. From this information, I can conclude that industrialized, more developed nations (MDCs) are located to the north of the Brandt Line and less developed nations (LDCs) are to the south. People living above the line would have a higher standard of living. They would live longer and have access to health care, clean water, sanitation, food, education, and consumer goods more often than those below the line. People would also work mainly in tertiary jobs that provide services in exchange for payment. Those living below the line would work mainly in primary jobs, and possible secondary ones. Their work often would be for trade or barter, rather than involving an exchange of money. Women would be subservient and not participate in what little education may be available.

Activity Seven—Cities and Urban Land Use

1) Identify and diagram the three models of urban structure that were discussed in Chapter 13.

2) Where would the most expensive housing be located in each? Where would the cheapest housing be located? Why? Are there any new trends in urbanization that might affect the most expensive and the cheapest housing?

Possible Answers:

1)   See FIGURES 13-5, 13-6 AND 13-7.

2)   In the Hoyt Sector Model and the Concentric Zone Model, the most expensive housing would be found in the outer most zones or sectors of the model. They would be farthest from the central business district. In the Multiple Nuclei model, however, expensive housing might be near the city center, but would not be in the same "node" as industry. In all three models, the cheapest housing would be located right next to the industrial zone/manufacturing area. The reason for this, is that the quality of life tends to go down the closer you get to factories, therefore, housing rents tend to be cheaper, so poorer people will live there. Some current trends in urbanization that might change these trends are gentrification and counterurbanization. Gentrified zones attract upper and middle class people because the inner city is revitalized and offers many services in a small area. People can move close to their jobs, save time on commuting, and have everything they want available to them. The same is true for counterurbanization, where people leave the cities and the suburbs to move to small rural communities. This movement is made possible due to globalization. Since we are all globally connected, a person who works on eBay for example, can be working from a rural farm and no one would be the wiser.

MULTIPLE CHOICE. Choose the one alternative that best completes the statement or answers the question.

1) 1:24,000 is an example of what kind of scale?
A) bar line
B) fractional scale
C) graphic scale
D) written scale
E) situational scale

2) Situation identifies a place by its
A) location relative to other objects.
B) mathematical location on Earth's surface.
C) nominal location.
D) unique physical characteristics.
E) unique cultural characteristics.

3) Site identifies a place by its
A) location relative to other objects.
B) mathematical location on Earth's surface.
C) nominal location.
D) unique physical characteristics.
E) unique cultural characteristics.

4) The concept that the distribution of one phenomenon is scientifically related to the location of other phenomena is
A) regional analysis.
B) spatial analysis.
C) spatial distortion.
D) spatial distribution.
E) spatial association.

5) One important feature of the world's population with the most significant future implications is that
A) it is increasing more slowly than in the past.
B) there are more people alive in the world now than at any time in the past.
C) the most rapid growth is occurring in the less developed countries.
D) people are uniformly distributed across Earth.
E) the most rapid growth is occurring in industrialized countries.

6) The world's population is clustered in four regions. Which of the following is not one of these four regions?
A) East Asia
B) Southeast Asia
C) Sub-Saharan Africa
D) Western Europe
E) Latin America

7) Physiological density is the number of
A) acres of farmland.
B) farmers per area of farmland.
C) people per area of land.
D) people per urban area
E) persons per area suitable for agriculture.

8) India and the United Kingdom have approximately the same arithmetic density. From this we can conclude that the two countries have the same
A) level of output per farmer.
B) number of people per area of land.
C) pressure placed by people on the land to produce food.
D) proportion of people living in cities
E) all of the above

9) The medical revolution has been characterized by
A) development of new inventions.
B) diffusion of medical practices.
C) increased agricultural productivity.
D) invention of new medicines.
E) discovery of medicinal plants in rainforest areas

10) The highest natural increase rates are found in countries in which stage of the demographic transition?
A) Stage 1
B) Stage 2
C) Stage 3
D) Stage 4
E) Stage 5

11) The percentage of people who are too young or too old to work in a society is the
A) total fertility rate.
B) life expectancy.
C) population pyramid.
D) sex ratio.
E) dependency rate.

12) The country with the narrowest population pyramid is
A) Cape Verde.
B) Chile.
C) Denmark.
D) the United States.
E) Mexico.

13) Thomas Malthus concluded that
A) population increased arithmetically while food production increased geometrically.
B) the world's rate of population increase was higher than the development of food supplies.
C) moral restraint was producing lower crude birth rates.
D) population growth was outpacing available resources in every country.
E) population was affecting our ability to find renewable resources.

14) Refugees migrate primarily because of which type of push factor?
A) economic
B) environmental
C) political
D) hunger
E) all of the above

15) Which of the following events would be considered a migration pull factor?
A) communist takeover of a government
B) failed harvest
C) flooding of a river

D) opening of a new factory
E) the bubonic plague

16) Millions of West Africans who migrated to Nigeria during the 1970s, when the country's economy expanded, were expelled during the 1980s, when the country's economy declined. This is an example of
A) an economic migration factor changing to an environmental migration factor.
B) emigration changing to immigration.
C) forced migration changing to voluntary migration.
D) a push factor changing to a pull factor.
E) a pull factor changing to a push factor.

17) Millions of Europeans were forced to emigrate from their farms because of
A) a decline in food supplies.
B) poor economic prospects in the rapidly growing cities.
C) forced consolidation of farms.
D) increased crude death rates.
E) increased crude birth rates.

18) Norwegians were most likely to immigrate to the United States
A) prior to 1840.
B) during the 1840s and 1850s.
C) during the 1880s and 1890s.
D) between 1900 and 1915.
E) none of the above.

19) Most Asians are currently migrating to the United States through the process of
A) boat people.
B) brain drain.
C) net migration.
D) illegal immigration.
E) chain migration

20) Counterurbanization is
A) the move from urban core to suburban areas.
B) due to expanding suburbs.
C) increased migration to rural areas and small towns.
D) the trend of the elderly retiring to rural locations.
E) the trend of young people becoming farmers.

21) Folk cultures are spread primarily by
A) contagious diffusion.
B) hierarchical diffusion.
C) relocation diffusion.
D) stimulus diffusion.
E) simultaneous diffusion.

22) The current distribution of soccer demonstrates that
A) a folk custom can become part of a popular culture.
B) all sports are examples of folk culture.
C) television has infused all sports into popular culture.
D) American football is also an example of a folk culture.
E) people are willing to pay money to Soccer players.

23) China produces a relatively large amount of pork compared to the countries of South Asia primarily because
A) Buddhists don't have a taboo against pork consumption.
B) its physical environment is more suitable to raising pigs.
C) China has more people than the countries of South Asia.
D) China believes that pork is healthier than beef.
E) all of the above

24) One significant impact of popular culture is to
A) create a more varied and less uniform landscape.
B) prevent the diffusion of folk culture.
C) prevent rapid industrialization
D) create more equity among nations.
E) modify the physical environment.

25) Many less developed countries fear the loss of folk culture because
A) they do not want to preserve traditional values.
B) Western perspectives may become more dominant.
C) popular cultural values can promote environmental damage.
D) they want to avoid political disputes.
E) none of the above.

26) As they have more contact with popular culture, women in less developed countries are more likely to
A) bear more children.
B) obtain food for the family.
C) gain more opportunities outside the home.
D) reduce the practice of prostitution.
E) become illiterate.

27) A literary tradition is
A) a form of a language used for official government business.
B) a form of a language spoken in a particular area.
C) a collection of languages related to each other.
D) a collection of oral histories.
E) the written form of a language.

28) A group of languages that share a common ancestor before recorded history is a
A) dialect.
B) language branch.
C) language family.
D) language group.
E) language sect.

29) When people who speak a given language migrate to a different location and become isolated from other members of their tribe
A) their language usually shows very little change even over a long period of time.
B) they immediately develop a literary tradition.
C) isolation usually results in the differentiation of one language into two.
D) they lose their linguistic abilities.
E) more people in the area they migrated to begin to speak the language.

30) A creolized language is
A) extinct.
B) a mix of indigenous and colonial languages.
C) an isolated language family.

D) a possible prehistoric superfamily.
E) begin taught in many schools.

31) The Flemings and Walloons speak languages belonging to different
A) dialects.
B) language branches.
C) language families.
D) language groups.
E) language sects.

32) With respect to the relationship between culture, religion, and the physical environment
A) few religions derive meaningful events from the physical environment.
B) religious ideas may be responsible for some of the changes people make in the physical environment.
C) religion is no longer an important source of identification for a distinct cultural group.
D) religion only deals with culture.
E) All of the above are true.

33) A large and fundamental division within a religion is a
A) cult.
B) denomination.
C) sect.
D) dialect.
E) branch.

34) A universalizing religion
A) is based on the physical characteristics of a particular location on Earth.
B) appeals to people living in a wide variety of locations.
C) is rarely transmitted through missionaries.
D) is intentionally developed to be a world religion.
E) is based on the Jewish calendar.

35) The world's largest universalizing religion is
A) Buddhism.
B) Christianity.
C) Hinduism.
D) Islam.
E) Shi'a.

36) The world's largest ethnic religion is
A) Confucianism.
B) Daoism.
C) Hinduism.
D) Shintoism.
E) Judaism.

37) Judaism is classified as an ethnic rather than a universalizing religion, primarily because
A) its main holidays relate to events in the life of its founder, Abraham.
B) it uses a lunar calendar.
C) its rituals derive from the agricultural cycle in Israel.
D) it commemorates the Exodus from Egypt.
E) it only uses the Old Testament.

38) Which is not a characteristic of a hierarchical religion?
A) It has a well-defined hierarchical structure.
B) It encourages each congregation to be self-sufficient.

C) It organizes territory into local administrative units.
D) It fosters interaction among different congregations.
E) It appeals to all religions.

39) Elements of nationalism include all but
A) common culture.
B) shared attitudes.
C) shared emotions.
D) patriotism.
E) political structure.

40) Denmark is a good example of a nation-state because
A) nearly all Danes speak Danish and live in Denmark.
B) Danish and German nationalities intermingle in Schleswig-Holstein.
C) the people living on the Faeroe islands, which are controlled by Denmark, speak Faeroese.
D) it was created as a result of the Treaty of Nantes.
E) all of the above

41) Balkanization refers to
A) the creation of nation-states in southeastern Europe.
B) the breakdown of a state due to conflicts among nationalities.
C) a small geographic area that cannot successfully be organized into states.
D) ethnic cleansing.
E) genocide.

42) Which of the following is not an element of cultural diversity?
A) language
B) religion
C) ethnicity
D) culture
E) race

43) Race is
A) characterized by Caucasian, African American, and Hispanic/Latino.
B) self-identification with a group sharing a biological ancestor.
C) determinable from physical characteristics.
D) evenly distributed around the world.
E) determinable from cultural characteristics.

44) A nation or nationality is
A) a group of people tied to a place through legal status and tradition.
B) a country.
C) ethnic identity.
D) any cohesive group of people.
E) a group of people tied together by culture.

45) Conflict in Africa is widespread because of
A) colonial boundaries.
B) numerous ethnic groups.
C) language differences.
D) tribal boundaries that were disrupted by colonial powers.
E) all of the above

46) The process when a group forcibly removes another group is called
A) war.
B) migrational push factors.
C) racism.
D) ethnic cleansing.
E) migrational pull factors.

47) One example of a multinational state is
A) Korea
B) Taiwan
C) United Kingdom
D) Iceland
E) Mexico

48) An area organized into an independent political unit is a
A) colony.
B) nationality.
C) satellite.
D) state.
E) common wealth.

49) A group of people who occupy a particular area and have a strong sense of unity based on a set of shared beliefs is a
A) centripetal force.
B) centrifugal force.
C) self-determination.
D) unitary state.
E) nation.

50) Over the past half century, the number of sovereign states in the world
A) has remained approximately the same.
B) has increased by a couple of dozen.
C) has decreased by a couple of dozen.
D) has increased by more than a hundred.
E) has decreased by more than a hundred.

51) Boundaries were redrawn in much of Europe after World War I according to the
A) distribution of languages.
B) demands of the victorious British and French.
C) containment of Nazism.
D) League of Nations.
E) physical environment.

52) With the end of the Cold War,
A) Russia has become a nation-state.
B) military alliances have become more important in Europe.
C) nationalities have been discouraged from expressing their cultural identities.
D) economic competition among regions has become more important than military competition.
E) competition among the regions has declined dramatically.

53) Which of the following conditions most affects the ability of some countries to participate in the global economy?
A) elongated.
B) perforated
C) large frontier

D) fragmented

E) landlocked

54) Development refers to

A) improvement in material conditions.

B) value of the output of goods and services.

C) value of a product compared to the needed labor.

D) division of jobs into different sectors.

E) decrease in CO2 emissions.

55) Per capita GDP is a good indicator of all but which of the following?

A) the approximate level of material well being in a country

B) the number of countries below the poverty level

C) the distribution of resources within a country

D) the spatial distribution of global wealth

E) the distribution of wealth within a country

56) An example of a primary sector activity is

A) education.

B) manufacturing.

C) mining.

D) retailing.

E) services.

57) Processing of computer information is an example of which sector of the economy?

A) primary

B) secondary

C) tertiary

D) quaternary

E) none of the above

58) Today, European countries obtain raw materials

A) from their abundant supplies.

B) through exploitation of their colonies.

C) through purchase from less developed countries.

D) access to raw materials is no longer important for development in Europe.

E) through purchase from more developed countries.

59) Compared to more developed countries, less developed countries typically have all but which of the following characteristics?

A) higher crude birth rates

B) lower dependency rates

C) higher percentage of children under age fifteen

D) lower percentage of elderly

E) lower percentage of children under age fifteen

60) Agricultural output in South Asia each year depends primarily on the

A) arrival of the monsoon.

B) diffusion of miracle seeds.

C) ratio between population and resources.

D) price of jute.

E) price of rice.

61) According to Rostow's development model, the process of development begins when
A) a high percentage of national wealth is allocated to nonproductive activities.
B) an elite group initiates innovative activities.
C) take-off industries achieve technical advances.
D) workers become more skilled and specialized.
E) none of the above.

62) In contrast to the international trade approach, the self-sufficiency approach to development
A) begins when an elite group initiates innovative activities.
B) results in uneven resource development.
C) suffers from market stagnation.
D) spreads investment only to the elite.
E) spreads investment through all sectors of the economy.

63) The most important distinction for dividing the world into agricultural regions is
A) whether the product is consumed on or off the farm.
B) whether crops are grown or animals are raised.
C) the location of the first agriculture.
D) the population density of the crop-producing region.
E) the amount of arable land available.

64) Unique agricultural practices arise in particular regions because of
A) characteristics of the physical environment.
B) limited knowledge of alternatives.
C) distinctive cultural traits.
D) cultural traditions about when to plant.
E) all of the above

65) Shifting cultivation causes environmental damage primarily when
A) population exceeds environmental capacity.
B) more fertilizers are introduced.
C) fields are permanently cleared.
D) cultural traditions are ignored.
E) less people are involved in farming.

66) Pastoral nomadism is most commonly found in which climate region?
A) humid low-latitude
B) dry
C) warm mid-latitude
D) cold mid-latitude
E) Mediterranean

67) To separate husks from seeds, Asian farmers beat the heads on the ground, a practice known as
A) chaff.
B) threshing.
C) winnowing.
D) double cropping.
E) triple cropping.

68) According to von Thünen's model, a commercial farmer is concerned with which of these costs?
A) price of land
B) cost of transporting output to market
C) value of yield per hectare
D) site factors
E) All of the above are considered.

69) Von Thünen's model can best be used to explain the location of which of the following types of agriculture?
A) dairying in the Northeast United States
B) ranching in the dry lands of North Africa
C) shifting cultivation in the tropics of South America
D) intensive subsistence in South China
E) cultivation in Nepal.

70) Unlike other forms of commercial agriculture, plantations are
A) part of agribusiness.
B) owned by people in less developed countries.
C) found primarily in less developed countries.
D) found primarily in developed countries.
E) all of the above

71) Prior to the Industrial Revolution, the distribution of industry was
A) clustered.
B) concentrated.
C) dispersed.
D) randomly distributed.
E) nonexistent

72) The most important transportation improvement in the eighteenth century was the
A) canal.
B) car.
C) railroad.
D) steam engine.
E) high speed train.

73) The growth of manufacturing was retarded in the United States during the nineteenth century primarily because of
A) abundant raw materials.
B) distance from markets.
C) labor surpluses.
D) labor unions.
E) all of the above

74) Copper concentration is a bulk-reducing industry, because
A) the mills are near the mines.
B) the final product has a much higher value per weight.
C) refineries import most material from other countries.
D) copper ore is low-grade.
E) mills are located south of the equator.

75) The location of a maquiladora plant is a good example of the importance of
A) situation factors.
B) NAFTA.
C) Post-Fordist production.
D) break-of-bulk points.
E) site factors.

76) A company which uses more than one mode of transport will often locate near
A) break-of-bulk points.
B) consumers.
C) raw materials.
D) suburbs.
E) rural areas.

77) In contrast to fordist production, Post-Fordist production is more likely to
A) follow Adam Smith's example.
B) place more importance on site factors.
C) assign each worker one task.
D) dominate transnational corporations.
E) introduce more flexible work rules.

78) The CBD attracts offices primarily because of its
A) high accessibility.
B) high land costs.
C) more intensive land use.
D) construction of skyscrapers.
E) isolation.

79) Land values are high in the CBD primarily because of
A) competition for limited space.
B) high threshold and range.
C) less intensive land use.
D) construction of skyscrapers.
E) fertile land.

80) Rural settlements differ from urban settlements primarily according to which type of activity?
A) cultural
B) economic
C) political
D) religious
E) leisure

81) The French long-lot system was developed primarily because of
A) collective land ownership.
B) common grazing land.
C) inheritance laws.
D) Enclosure Act.
E) need for access to a river.

82) The most significant anticipated benefit of the enclosure movement was to
A) destroy traditional village life.
B) promote agricultural efficiency.
C) replace abandoned villages with new farmsteads.
D) stimulate urbanization.
E) gain access to a river.

83) The typical medieval European urban settlements were characterized by the
A) dispersal of palaces, churches, and other important buildings throughout the town.
B) placement of farms surrounded by walls.
C) demolition of ancient walls surrounding the town.
D) provision of parks and open space surrounding important churches.
E) placement of buildings around a central market square.

84) The maximum distance people are willing to travel for a service is
A) hinterland.
B) range.
C) threshold.
D) median.
E) maximum.

85) According to the gravity model, the potential use of a service at a location is related
A) directly to population and inversely to distance.
B) directly to distance and inversely to population.
C) directly to both population and distance.
D) inversely to both distance and population.
E) inversely to number of people per square mile.

86) If a country's largest city has 1,000,000 inhabitants and the second largest city has 200,000 inhabitants, the country follows what distribution?
A) central place
B) economic base
C) primate city
D) rank-size
E) Von Thunen's model

87) Which statement best describes the relationship between urbanization and the Industrial Revolution?
A) Urbanization promoted the Industrial Revolution.
B) The Industrial Revolution promoted agricultural practices.
C) Urbanization preceded the Industrial Revolution by thousands of years.
D) Urbanization and the Industrial Revolution are no longer related.
E) The Industrial Revolution promoted urbanization.

88) In the United States, which of the following definitions of a city covers the largest land area?
A) central business district
B) central city
C) urbanized area
D) metropolitan statistical area
E) rank size

89) The process of change in the use of a house, from single-family owner occupancy to abandonment, is
A) blockbusting.
B) filtering.
C) gentrification.
D) redlining.
E) redistricting

90) Public transit is more extensive in Western European cities than in the United States primarily because
A) Europeans can't afford cars.
B) European governments subsidize public transit.
C) density is lower.
D) the central city contains fewer high-rises.
E) Americans want to own cars

91) According to the concentric zone model, a city develops in a series of
A) corridors.
B) nodes.
C) rings.
D) all of the above
E) none of the above

92) According to the sector model, the best housing is located in
A) a corridor from the suburbs to the farms.
B) an outer ring surrounding the city.
C) nodes near universities and parks.
D) renovated inner-city neighborhoods.
E) a corridor from downtown to the edge of the city.

93) According to the multiple nuclei model, an airport is likely to attract nearby
A) industries.
B) residences.
C) shops.
D) universities.
E) colleges.

94) Compared to the United States, poor families in European cities are more likely to be
A) clustered in inner-city neighborhoods.
B) dispersed throughout the city.
C) clustered in suburbs.
D) distributed uniformly in the city.
E) dispersed in the inner-cities.

95) Most nonrenewable energy sources are
A) replaced continually.
B) formed rapidly.
C) never replenished.
D) a potential reserve.
E) formed very slowly

96) The best example of a country that consumes more energy than it produces is
A) China.
B) Japan.
C) Saudi Arabia.
D) the United Kingdom.
E) the United States.

97) From the mid-1970s until the mid-1980s, the main policy of OPEC was to
A) raise the price of petroleum.
B) refuse to sell petroleum to the United States.
C) nationalize American-owned petroleum companies.
D) gain more members.
E) all of the above

98) An atmospheric condition in which sunlight causes nitrogen oxides to react in the atmosphere is
A) acid deposition.
B) chlorofluorocarbon.
C) greenhouse effect.
D) photochemical smog.
E) inversion effect.

99) An alternative to reducing discharges into the environment is
A) changing the mix of inputs increasing the product to waste ratio.
B) using the waste in the same production process.
C) using the waste in a different production process.
D) using the environment more efficiently.
E) none of the above.

100) Critics and defenders of sustainable development both agree that
A) definitions of resources change drastically and unpredictably over time.
B) earth has only 11.4 billion hectares of biologically productive land.
C) less international cooperation is needed to reduce the gap between LDCs and MDCs.
D) isolationist policies are the best approach.
E) more international cooperation is needed to reduce the gap between LDCs and MDCs.

Free-Response Questions

Unit II: Population

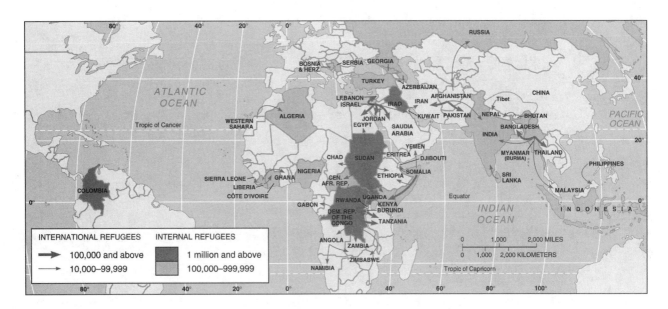

Figure 3-1 Major sources and destinations of refugees.

A. Define the following terms as they are used in population geography:

a) refugee

b) push and pull factors

c) international and internal migration

d) voluntary and forced migration

B. According to the map above, which countries have the highest number of internal refugees, and in which regions are the major flows of international refugees?

C. Explain the major push and pull factors for any one country on the map that has a large number of internal and/or international refugees.

Unit III: Cultural Patterns and Processes

A. What is the difference between folk and popular culture? Give one specific example of each.

B. Identify and describe the types of diffusion associated with popular culture.

C. Give two reasons why popular culture may cause problems, and illustrate each with a specific example.

Unit IV: Political Organization of Space

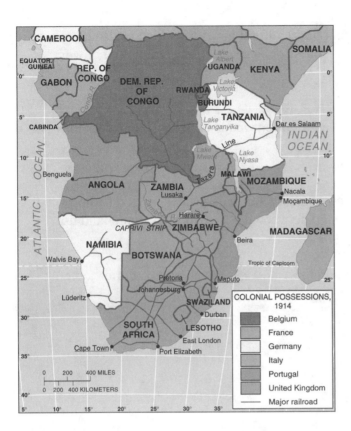

Figure 8-6 Southern Africa

A. Define the following terms as they are used in political geography:

a) fragmented state

b) perforated state

c) prorupted state

d) superimposed boundary

B. Name specific examples of fragmented, perforated, and prorupted states from the map above, and explain why most of the boundaries shown on that map are examples of superimposed boundaries.

C. Give two principal reasons for the creation of proruptions in general, and give a specific reason for the creation of one of the proruptions shown on the map above.

Unit V: Agriculture and Rural Land Use

With reference to Von Thünen's model of agricultural land use, which is also known as *The Isolated State*, answer the following question. Use specific examples wherever appropriate.

A. Diagram the model and identify two assumptions made by Von Thünen that may not be true in reality.

B. According to the model, what two costs must a farmer consider when deciding which crops to cultivate? What is the relationship between distance to market and land use?

C. To what extent is the model relevant in more and less developed countries today?

Unit VI: Industrialization and Development

The Human Development Index (HDI), created by the United Nations, recognizes that a country's level of development is a function of economic, social, and demographic factors.

A. Within the economic factor of development, what categories of jobs does the HDI recognize, and how is the distribution of workers in these categories an indication of level of development?

B. Identify three demographic indicators of development, and briefly explain how each can help to determine the level of development of a country.

C. Select a specific country that has a very high HDI, and outline an economic, social, and demographic characteristic that helps to identify it as such.

D. Select a specific country that has a low HDI, and outline an economic, social, and demographic characteristic that helps to identify it as such.

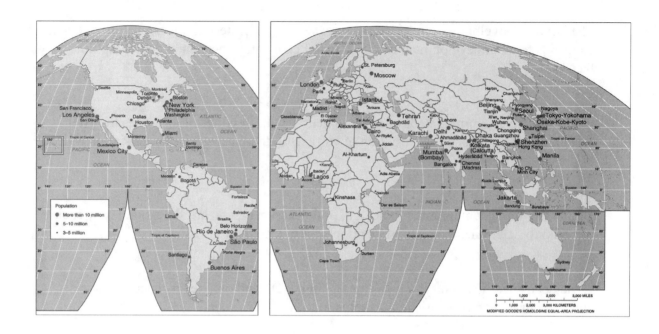

Figure 13-2 Cities having a population of 2 million or more.

A. What is the difference between the primate city rule and the rank-size rule? For each of these concepts, name a specific example from the map above.

B. Briefly discuss two reasons why London, New York, and Tokyo are considered the most important of the world cities.

C. Briefly discuss two reasons why there is a much more rapid growth of cities in LDCs than in MDCs today.

Answers to Multiple Choice Examination Questions

1. **B**-numerical ration between distances on the map and the Earth's surface.
2. **A**-Situation is the location of a place relative to other places.
3. **D**-site is the physical character of a place.
4. **E**-Association of a certain situation (like cancer rates) distributed at various scales.---SEE FIGURE 1-13.
5. **C**-these countries are at stage 2 of the demographic transition zone and have not yet entered an industrial revolution. They continue to have many children and growth increases in LDC's exacerbate the stresses felt in those places.
6. **D**-The four regions include East Asia, Southeast Asia, Western Europe and South Asia.
7. **E**-physiological density is the number of people supported by a unit area of arable land.
8. **B**-arithmetic density is the total number of people divided by the total land area.
9. **B**-medical revolution spreads medical technology (like anti-malaria drugs) around the globe.
10. **B**-Stage 2 means that the difference in crude birth rate and crude death rate is very high so therefore the rate of natural increase is high. (CBR 35-CDR 5=RNI 30)
11. **E**
12. **C**-Denmark is at stage 4 of growth, with the percentage of young people and old people nearly the same.
13. **B**-Malthus wrote "An Essay on the Principle of Population (1798)" state that population grows geometrically and food supply increases arithmetically.
14. **C**-refugees are people who have been forced to migrate from their home and cannot return for fear of persecution.
15. **D**-pull factors induce people to new locations, such as economic incentives (jobs).
16. **E**-people were pulled to be guest workers and were pushed out when jobs ran out.
17. **C**-The Enclosure movement was a governmental policy to make farming more efficient.
18. **C**-The Industrial Revolution had diffused into these countries and population increased, this made it difficult to find farm land, so people immigrated in search of land.
19. **E**-Chain migration is the migration of people to a specific place because relatives or members of the same nationality live there.
20. **C**-counterurbanization is net migration from urban to rural areas.
21. **C**-relocation diffusion is the spread of a characteristic through migration.
22. **A**-Organization of the sport into a formal structure with uniform rules that are followed globally, made soccer transform from a folk culture to a popular culture.

23. **A**-Muslims and Jews have food taboos against pork.
24. **E**-popular culture is dependent on a high level of economic development to acquire material wealth. This disrupts the physical environment with increases in pollution, trash, and also building of sports arenas, malls etc…
25. **B**-people turn away from their society's traditional values.
26. **C**-women will lose their subservience to men. This may allow them access to education and work, or this may have negative impacts like the increase in prostitution.
27. **E**-literary tradition is language that is written as well as spoken.
28. **C**
29. **C**
30. **B**
31. **B**-Walloons speak French and the Flemings speak a dialect of the Germanic language of Dutch (Flemish).
32. **B**-like in their response to sacred places (Mecca), places of worship (churches, cathedrals), burial practices or toponymns.
33. **E**
34. **B**-universalizing religion attempts to be global and appeal to all people.
35. **B**-Christianity has two billion followers.
36. **C**-Hinduism has 860 million followers.
37. **C**-The Jewish calendar's major holidays are based on the agricultural calendar of Israel.
38. **B**-hierarchical religion has a well defined geographic structure and organizes territory into local administrative units (Roman Catholic Church) encouraging interaction among the units.
39. **E**-nationalism is loyalty and devotion to a particular nationality.
40. **A**-nation-state is a territory that corresponds to a particular ethnicity.
41. **B**-break up of an area, sometimes referred to as devolution.
42. **E**
43. **B**
44. **A**
45. **E**-colonial boundaries were drawn with regard to ethnic groups (tribes) or culture (especially language) SEE MAP 7-23.
46. **D**
47. **C**-The United Kingdom is made up of England, Scotland, Wales and Northern Ireland
48. **D**-sometimes the word, state, is used synonymously for country.
49. **E**
50. **D**-most of this has occurred due to countries obtaining independence from a colonial power, especially in Africa, as well as the break up of the Soviet Union and Yugoslavia.
51. **A**-Woodrow Wilson and Isaiah Bowman decided that language was the easiest way to redraw the map of Europe after the break up of the Ottoman Empire.
52. **D**-the end of the Cold War created the need for economic alliances.
53. **E**-Africa has 14 landlocked countries out of its 54.

54. **A**-development is a process of improvement in the material condition of people through the diffusion of knowledge and technology.

55. **E**-per capita GDP is the value of the total output of goods and services produced in a country during a normal year divided by the total population of the country.

56. **C**-primary sector jobs directly extract materials from the Earth

57. **C**-tertiary jobs involve the provision of goods and services to people in exchange for payment

58. **C**

59. **D**-dependency rate is the number of people under 15 and over 65 compared to the number of people in the work force

60. **A**-the majority of people are involved in subsistence agriculture and have little technology, so the monsoon brings needed rain for cultivation

61. **B**-under Rostow's model a country will go through five stages of development. Stage 2 is known as the precondition for take off when an elite group emerges.

62. **E**-also called the balanced growth approach.

63. **A**-this is also aligned with LDC's and MDC's. In LDC's subsistence agriculture occurs and most food is consumed on the farm, in MDC's it is commercial agriculture where cash crops are produced and sent to market.

64. **E**

65. **A**-shifting agriculture occurs in humid low latitudes with high temperatures and abundant rainfall. Land cleared (swidden) is only fertile for about three years. Where population increases, more land must be cleared.

66. **B**-drylands of North Africa and Asia. SEE FIGURE 10-5

67. **B**

68. **E**-Johann H. von Thünen wrote "The Isolated State." SEE FIGURE 10-13

69. **A**-dairy farming would occur near population hubs where transportation is efficient and quick, as dairy products are perishable items.

70. **C**-plantations were set up by colonial powers (MDC's) to gain cash crops.

71. **C**-people made household tools and farm equipment in their own home.

72. **A**-canals allowed goods and workers to move long distance more efficiently and faster.

73. **B**-the distance from the market and poor transportation made manufacturing less lucrative in the US

74. **B**-bulk-reducing industries are economic activities in which the final product actually weighs less than its inputs.

75. **E**-site factors no longer focus on location near raw materials but rather on factors of production: land, labor, capital.

76. **A**-Break-of-bulk points are locations where transfer among transportation modes is possible.

77. **E**-Fordist production was when a skilled laborer repeated the same task over and over again, Post-Fordist was when skilled workers were in teams and worked on a variety of tasks.

78. **A**-CBD(central business district) is an area of a city where retail and office activities are clustered.
79. **A**-CBD is prime location therefore the land rent is high.
80. **B**-the type of economic activity varies from urban areas.
81. **E**-SEE FIGURE 12-4.
82. **B**-The Enclosure Movement (1750-1850) consolidated individually owned land surrounding villages into one single farm.
83. **E**-SEE FIGURES 12-12 AND 12-13.
84. **B**
85. **A**-In order to maximize profits your location must minimize distance to the service for the largest number of people.
86. **C**-primate city rule is that the largest settlement has more than twice as many people as the second ranking settlement.
87. **E**-people moved to the cities for jobs.
88. **D**-the US Census Bureau's method of measuring the functional area of a city.
89. **B**
90. **B**-SEE FIGURE 13-22
91. **C**-SEE FIGURE 13-5
92. **E**-Hoyt believed that as a city grew, activity would expand outward in a wedge (sector) from the center and high valued house would emerge in this sector.
93. **A**-this model adheres to the geographic principle of agglomeration.
94. **C**-where as wealthy Europeans still live in elegant houses within the city center.
95. **E**-these would be fossil fuels and nuclear energy.
96. **B**-Japan lacks natural resources and is therefore dependent on importing fuel from other countries.
97. **A**-OPEC's policy is to manipulate the supply of petroleum in order to adjust the price paid per barrel.
98. **D**-this causes heavy smog and health problems.
99. **D**-recycling, wasting less and reducing consumption.
100. **E**-SEE FIGURE 14-16, development and environmental concerns are directly tied together.

Answers to Free-Response Questions

Unit II: Population

A. a) Refugees are people who are forced to flee their homeland and who are afraid to return for fear of persecution because of race, religion, nationality, or political opinion.

b) Push factors make people move out of their present location. Push factors are economic, cultural, and environmental, and include war, famine, and political instability. Pull factors attract people to a new location, and they can also be economic, cultural, and environmental. People are often enticed to a new place because of a job.

c) International migration is the permanent movement of people from one country to another. Internal migration is the permanent movement of people within a country.

d) Voluntary migration is permanent migration done through choice, such as relocation for a new and better job. Forced migration on the other hand is not by choice but rather forced for cultural reasons, such as war and ethnic cleansing.

B. The countries with the largest number of internal refugees are Colombia, Sudan, Uganda, Rwanda, the Democratic Republic of the Congo, and Iraq. The major flows of international refugees are in central and eastern Africa, the Middle East, and from Afghanistan and Myanmar to neighboring countries.

C. Sudan is an interesting example of both internal and international refugees, all due to war. As a result of the civil war, many people have been pushed out of Sudan to refugee camps in Uganda, Kenya, and Chad. Today, with the crisis in Darfur (western Sudan), many people are fleeing to other parts of Sudan as well as Chad.

Unit III: Cultural Patterns and Practices

A. Folk culture is practiced by a relatively homogeneous group, in a fairly isolated region, and is very slow to spread. The Amish culture is a good example. Popular culture is global and is spread throughout a heterogeneous group on a very large scale. It spreads quickly as a result of modern technology. Examples of popular culture are blue jeans and fast food restaurants.

B. Popular culture spreads through expansion diffusion, which is a snowballing process. There are three types of expansion diffusion, all of which can be associated with popular culture. Hierarchical diffusion spreads from nodes of authority. Contagious diffusion is the rapid, widespread diffusion of an innovation through the population. Stimulus

131

diffusion is the spread of an underlying principle even if the characteristic itself doesn't diffuse.

C. Popular culture may cause problems because an area loses its local diversity, such as giving up a native language to speak English. People may give up traditional values and adopt "Western" ways of doing things. Popular culture is based on consumerism and material gain, and thus can pollute the environment through needless packaging or the building of a golf course in a desert.

Unit IV: Political Organization of Space

A. a) A fragmented state includes several separate pieces of land that are not together.

b) A perforated state has a hole in it; it completely surrounds another state(s).

c) A prorupted state is a compact state with an extension coming out from it.

d) Superimposed boundaries are created by powerful outsiders, such as the boundaries created by colonial powers.

B. Angola is an example of a fragmented state. South Africa is perforated, and Namibia is a prorupted state. All of these boundaries were imposed by European colonial powers.

C. A proruption can separate two countries that would otherwise share a boundary. Thus it can prevent adjacent boundaries between countries. Proruptions are also created to provide access to a resource such as water. The Caprivi Strip (which is now part of Namibia) gave German colonists access to the Zambezi River in southern Africa in territory that would otherwise have been part of Britain's African empire. It may have also contributed to the disruption of British communications in the region.

Unit V: Agriculture and Rural Land Use

A. Von Thünen's model of agricultural land use has a city at the center surrounded by a ring of horticulture and dairy farming. Outside that ring is one of forestry, which in turn is surrounded by one of crop rotation, and agriculture that becomes more extensive the further one goes from the city. The ring that is furthest from the city is one of grazing. The model assumes that this is a uniform plain with no variation in physical geography. Von Thünen also assumed that there is equal ease of transportation in all directions.

B. A farmer must consider the cost of land, and the cost of transporting products to market. The relationship between distance to market and land use is critical because the cost of transporting each product is different. A farmer might choose a crop that does not yield as much profit per acre because transportation costs for the product are cheaper.

C. Even though the land use pattern around a city in the developed world no longer looks like this, the underlying principles are still the same. For example agricultural land use will always be more intensive closer to the market and more extensive the further one gets from a city. The cost of land and the cost of transporting goods to market are still critical.

The agricultural land use pattern around many cities in the developing world may still closely resemble the model. These regions do not have modern technology, such as refrigerated dairy containers, so the dairy ring must remain close to the city. Wood is a major building and fuel supplier in many of these countries. The land use pattern around Addis Ababa, Ethiopia, is much the same as von Thünen's original model.

In both the developed and developing worlds, explanations of the differences between reality and the model will enhance one's understanding of agricultural land use.

Unit VI: Industrialization and Development

A. The HDI recognizes jobs in the primary, secondary, and tertiary sectors of the economy. As a country becomes more developed, the percentage of workers in the primary sector will decline as the percentage in the secondary sector increases. Today more developed countries (MDCs) have the largest percentage of workers in the tertiary sector of the economy. The percentage of workers in agriculture is more than 60% in less developed countries (LDCs) and less than 5% in MDCs.

B. In more developed countries (MDCs), life expectancy is higher because people have better access to health care. The infant mortality rate is also much higher in less developed countries (LDCs) for the same reasons. The rate of natural increase is higher in LDCs, which puts a great strain on their resources. Cultural practices and a lack of education with regard to birth control contribute to such high rates of natural increase, especially in Sub-Saharan Africa.

C. Japan has a very high HDI. The majority of people in this country work in the tertiary sector of the economy. Japanese people are generally very educated, and have access to quality health care. Life expectancy is around 80 years.

Afghanistan has a very low HDI. The people in this country work in the primary sector of the economy as farmers or pastoral nomads. Most Afghans do not have access to education; therefore literacy rates are very low. They have a low life expectancy, and a high crude birthrate.

Unit VII: Cities and Urban Land Use

A. According to the primate city rule, the largest city in a country has twice as many people as the second-largest city. Moscow is a primate city in Russia because it is twice as large as St. Petersburg. The rank-size rule explains the pattern of settlements in a country where the nth largest settlement is 1/nth the population of the largest settlement. The relative size of settlements in Brazil and the United States follow the rank-size rule more than the primate city rule. Neither of these countries have one primate city, although the extent to which they follow the rank-size rule is still difficult to determine from the map.

B. London, New York, and Tokyo are the most important of the world cities because they are much larger and more important than any other cities in their respective regions. All three are home to the world's most important stock exchanges. They all also contain larger concentrations of financial and business services than other cities in the world.

C. Population growth is much more rapid in LDCs than MDCs today. Cities are also growing much faster in LDCs. Much of this is the result of push factors in rural areas. Agriculture is collapsing in many developing regions and people are moving to urban areas in search of work. This is particularly true in Latin America, where slums are growing on the outskirts of major metropolitan areas.
The migration trend in MDCs for the last few decades has been from urban to suburban areas. Edge cities have been created on the suburban fringe of many North American cities. Counterurbanization, or the movement from urban to rural communities, has been a growing trend in the last decade in the more developed world.